Juggling

From Start to Star

Dave, Dorothy, and Ben Finnigan

Human Kinetics

Library of Congress Cataloging-in-Publication Data

Finnigan, Dave.
   Juggling: from start to star / Dave, Dorothy, and Ben Finnigan.
    p. cm.
   ISBN 0-7360-3750-0
   1. Juggling. I. Finnigan, Dorothy, 1984- II. Finnigan, Ben, 1988- III. Title.
   GV1558 .F57 2001
   793.8'7--dc21

                                                         00-054238

ISBN: 0-7360-3750-0

Developmental Editor: Laura Hambly
Assistant Editors: Kim Thoren and Stephan Seyfert
Copyeditor: Patsy Fortney
Proofreader: Pam Johnson
Graphic Designer: Fred Starbird
Photo Manager: Clark Brooks
Cover Designer: Keith Blomberg
Photographer (cover and interior): Tom Roberts, unless otherwise noted
Illustrator: Mic Greenberg
Printer: Bang Printing

Human Kinetics books are available at special discounts for bulk purchase. Special editions or book excerpts can also be created to specification. For details, contact the Special Sales Manager at Human Kinetics.

Printed in the United States of America
10 9 8 7 6 5 4 3 2 1

Human Kinetics
Web site: www.humankinetics.com

United States: Human Kinetics
P.O. Box 5076
Champaign, IL 61825-5076
800-747-4457
e-mail: humank@hkusa.com

Canada: Human Kinetics
475 Devonshire Road Unit 100
Windsor, ON N8Y 2L5
800-465-7301 (in Canada only)
e-mail: hkcan@mnsi.net

Europe: Human Kinetics
Units C2/C3 Wira Business Park
West Park Ring Road
Leeds LS16 6EB, United Kingdom
+44 (0) 113 278 1708
e-mail: hk@hkeurope.com

Australia: Human Kinetics
57A Price Avenue
Lower Mitcham, South Australia 5062
08 8277 1555
e-mail: liahka@senet.com.au

New Zealand: Human Kinetics
P.O. Box 105-231, Auckland Central
09-523-3462
e-mail: hkp@ihug.co.nz

This book is dedicated:

To Rosie O'Donnell, Oprah Winfrey, Regis Philbin, Jay Leno, David Letterman, and their successors, who follow in the footsteps of Ed Sullivan, Steve Allen, and Johnny Carson and have the power to keep juggling alive and in the public eye.

To the physical educators and recreation specialists who had the foresight to introduce juggling and circus arts even though these subjects were not yet a recognized part of the curriculum.

And to Thelma, Davy, and our friends all over the world who share the joy of juggling.

Contents

List of Skills

Preface

This book is designed to be the easiest and most straightforward juggling instruction manual ever written. It is intended for anyone interested in juggling, regardless of age or previous juggling experience. It is written step by step to cover a broad spectrum of juggling skills with precise detail, from the very basic through intermediate and advanced skills. Slow-moving nylon scarves build confidence and make learning the basic patterns so easy that you will see success in your first practice session. From there you can move on to beanbags, balls, rings, and clubs in a natural progression. Once you've learned the basics of toss juggling, you can also try your hand at the other juggling props covered in the book, including devil sticks, diabolos, spinning plates and balls, cigar boxes, and hats. For the brave of heart, there are even special sections that cover unicycle riding and torch juggling.

This book is unique because it was written by three members of a family who are all professional juggling teachers and experienced performers. As such, we are able to offer lessons from both an instructor's and a performer's perspective. This book is designed for both complete beginners and experienced jugglers who want to expand and improve their repertoires. The list of skills that follows the table of contents will make it easy to find specific moves that you want to learn. Detailed instructions and tips are provided so that you can practice a move, execute it well, and fit it into an overall routine. The performance tips, which feature a star design, provide information for improving skill presentation and audience appeal. The learning tips, indicated by a ring design, are designed to make it easier to learn specific skills by approaching the instruction from a different point of view.

If you are a beginner, you can start at page 1 and work your way through the book one chapter at a time. Everything is presented in order of difficulty, with basic skills that form your building blocks presented first, and more complex skills presented only after the fundamentals have been covered. If you are an intermediate or advanced juggler, start wherever you feel comfortable, but you may want to read over the tips in previous sections to make certain you are not missing any vital information that might improve your existing patterns or help polish your style. Now get ready to use both sides of your body and both halves of your brain as we go together "from Start to Star."

chapter

1

Juggling Fundamentals

Juggling is a physically challenging and mentally relaxing form of recreation that helps you discover and nurture your innate rhythm, coordination, poise, and agility. It reinforces patience, persistence, focus, and concentration while also improving self-confidence. Sounds great, right? So why aren't we all jugglers? Many people believe that it takes extraordinary coordination to master this ancient art. Not true. We have taught more than one million people to juggle, from very young children to seniors. What did they all have in common? Persistence, not coordination. They all learned the same way, drop by drop and step by step. So don't hesitate to drop. Just remember, "A drop is a sign of progress!"

Unlike most sports, juggling is a portable activity requiring very little equipment and no special playing space. Once you learn the skill, you can get up in front of others and perform, so it can be great for enhancing stage presence and improving self-esteem. It is a wonderful skill to share. Almost everyone wants to learn to juggle—they just need to know how to get started. This is where this book comes in. Juggling is an "equal opportunity activity," since girls and boys, young and old, athletes and those with no athletic experience can all succeed with a little practice.

Choosing Props

Once you know the basics, you can juggle any three objects that you can toss from hand to hand. However, before you break out the chainsaws or live animals, it's best to stick with traditional props such as scarves, balls, rings, and clubs, until you've got them mastered. In this section we describe toss juggling props and where to find them. Once you're ready to move on to other props, such as devil sticks, diabolos, or spinning balls, you can turn to those chapters for advice on what to buy.*

● *Scarves*—Until scarves came along, juggling was a skill reserved mainly for teenagers and adults. Children as young as five or six can now learn to juggle three colorful and slow-moving nylon scarves. No matter what your age or previous athletic experience, we strongly recommend starting with scarves to learn the patterns and the timing of juggling. Then, as coordination and reflexes improve, go on in a natural progression to beanbags, which don't bounce away when dropped, and then to balls, which do. Once you are comfortable with beanbags and balls, you can go on to rings and then to clubs. Because they present a bigger target than balls, scarves are much easier to catch. The only difference in technique is that you juggle scarves with your palms down and balls with your palms up. Remember that you can always go back to scarves to learn a new move or to add comedy to a performance.

● *Beanbags and Balls*—When you do move beyond scarves, look for round, no-bounce beanbags with a good grip. Jugglebug makes the perfect beginner item, JuggleBeanBalls, combining the best features of both a beanbag and a ball. Each set has three colors, and the balls are numbered to make it easy to remember the order in which you throw. They are washable and extremely durable, are made of plastic and stuffed with plastic pellets, and have no sewn seams. Once you are ready to try your hand with a bouncy ball, try Jugglebug's Professor Confidence set of three professional-quality balls. Avoid lightweight balls such as tennis balls and bouncy rubber balls when you are trying to learn. You need a ball that sinks into your hand when you catch it, but won't bounce away when it is dropped. It helps to have different colors so that you can see the place-ment of each ball in the pattern.

● *Rings*—Rings generally come next and are pretty standard: 13 inches in outside diameter so that they can slip easily over your head.

● *Clubs*—Next come clubs, and here there is tremendous variety. You can start with a beginner set of clubs for around $25 for three, or soft and

---

*You can find beginner sets of every prop described in this book at your local magic store, at most kite shops or high-quality toy stores, and on our Web site: **www.jugglebug.com**. You may also want to look at the section at the back of this book called "Where to Go for More Information."

safe foam clubs for under $40, or you can spend up to $120 per set. We certainly suggest starting with less expensive clubs and moving up to a more professional set only after you have learned a few basic patterns and want to start passing. Many prop makers can be found on the Internet, and links to all of them can be found at **www.jugglebug.com**.

Perfect Practice Makes Perfect

Once you have decided to learn to juggle, a few fundamentals will make learning easier. First, remember that whatever you practice is what you learn. If you practice a sloppy or incorrect move, it will become a habit and a barrier to further progress. Make sure you practice steps correctly when you are learning a new skill.

Learn to use both hands equally. Very few juggling patterns are asymmetrical. Since your dominant hand—the one you write with—learns more quickly, concentrate on your nondominant hand.

One of the most important things to understand about toss juggling is that, no matter what props you are using, the action generally takes place in a two-dimensional plane in front of you, using height and width, but not depth, as shown in figure 1.1. You avoid collisions not by shoveling in toward yourself, but by scooping from side to side, as if you are tossing under a microphone in front of your face. You need two peaks at the same height, one on each side. Reach up now and establish two targets in the air. When you start, these peaks can be two feet or more over each shoulder, but as you become proficient, you can bring them down, juggling faster and lower, or you can take them in or out,

Figure 1.1 Juggling takes place in a flat plane in front of you, using height and width, but not depth.

narrowing and widening your pattern. Explore the space in front of you as if it were a big picture frame that you need to fill with juggling.

When you first start to juggle, your feet should be about shoulder-width apart, with your weight equally distributed. Try to stay in one place when you are first learning. If you find yourself running forward or scooping in toward yourself, remember that everything happens on an imaginary wall in front of you. Avoid the temptation to try juggling against a real wall since bouncing against the wall will make you dependent on it and just pull you forward.

Practice in a nice place where weather, a ringing phone, or spectators are not an impediment. When practicing with scarves, you need to be inside because of the wind. With beanbags or balls you might want to start your practice over your bed so that you don't have to bend over constantly to pick up objects. Also, practicing over the bed can help you to keep everything in a flat plane in front of you since you don't have the option of running forward. Under a palm tree on Maui is our favorite spot to practice, but that isn't often an option for most of us.

Put on some music with an appropriate beat. For scarves this may mean slower classical music, old time rock 'n' roll, or mellow swing tunes. For balls you may want to try reggae or ragtime or faster big band numbers. For clubs, experiment with rock, fast jazz, or a powerful symphonic overture. Avoid music without a decided beat, such as music with long guitar riffs or modern jazz, until you are a proficient juggler. You want the music to assist you in establishing a rhythm.

Remember that everyone learns to juggle drop by drop. How long you practice each time depends on your environment, your stamina, and your innate love of challenges. If you set up your practice sessions correctly, you will be in a nice space with pleasant music and no disturbances, so you will want to practice. For some of you juggling will become an obsession, consuming five or six hours every day as you whip through this book and any other material you can find. However, taking two 15-minute juggling breaks a day instead of smoke breaks or coffee breaks may be your optimum. No matter how much you practice, be easy on yourself. Two phrases will help you to persevere: *A drop is a sign of progress*, and *A touch is as good as a catch*.

Don't just juggle until you drop one of your objects and then quit the session. Get in the habit of finishing cleanly. Choose a number of repetitions at which to stop or change your pattern and then do exactly that number. Charting your progress helps right from the start. Keep track of the number of tosses and successful catches you make for any move you are learning, and push yourself to complete at least one more catch with every attempt. If you are working on the reverse cascade with three balls, for example, and you do seven tosses and catches today, try for ten or twelve tomorrow. By setting these daily goals, you will get to see your progress; you can even reward yourself for reaching goals: "As soon as I get 100 tosses with three clubs, I'm going to get a banana split."

Stay relaxed while practicing. Keep breathing; don't hold your breath. Your shoulders should be relaxed, not hunched up. Resist the temptation to speed up your juggling patterns. If you find yourself repeating the same error over and over, stop at the exact moment of the error, close your eyes, and think about what you were trying to do. See it correctly in your mind's eye. Figure out what you need to do to correct the error, open your eyes, and try again. Don't repeat errors until they become bad habits and obstacles to progress. You can always go back and repeat a previous step until it is perfected and then move forward again.

Use verbal cues to push yourself. If you say "over, over, over" while tossing the balls or scarves in a reverse cascade, you will tend to do what you say and throw over. Also, use positive self-talk to help yourself learn. Visualize your success. If you are working on a move, visualize it just before you go to sleep at night and you will find improvement in the morning.

If possible, become a gregarious juggler. Find your local juggling club, or start one. Working with others can be a great source of inspiration, and you can check on one another's progress. Use the buddy system in order to avoid establishing bad habits. As soon as you have a credible cascade, go to your nearest local juggling festival, or even to the annual IJA festival, and take all the workshops that are offered. The more you hang out with other jugglers, the faster you will progress. When you are with other jugglers, don't hesitate to try new skills. No juggler will ever think badly of you as long as you are trying to learn. We all know that the only difference between a good juggler and a great juggler is practice.

History of Juggling

Juggling is an ancient art. The first graphic representations of three-ball jugglers that have been preserved appear on the wall paintings of the Beni-Hassan tombs on the east bank of the Nile, dating from 2600 B.C. Scrolls over 4,500 years old tell us that encamped soldiers in ancient China practiced manipulating spears and tridents. Still in the pre-Christian era, Roman legionnaire Sidonious Apollinaris is known to have entertained his troops by juggling three balls. By the sixth century A.D., wandering "jongleurs" juggled balls and knives throughout the French and English countryside. For four centuries, from the time of William the conqueror in 1066, the title "King of the Jugglers" was conferred by statute on the most esteemed palace entertainer in England.

Juggling declined throughout Europe during and after the Second World War. However, a revival of juggling as recreation started in Britain, France, and Germany in the late 1970s. Now the annual European juggling festival, held in a different country each year in August or early September, draws crowds of up to 4,000 recreational and performing jugglers from every country in Europe.

In the United States and Canada juggling reached its most recent zenith during the vaudeville era, when virtually every show had a juggler on the bill. After the decline of vaudeville, circuses and magic shows, street performers, and renaissance fairs barely kept the skill alive, but juggling was often regarded as a "secret art" like magic. Juggling was gradually restored to popularity by the International Jugglers Association (IJA), which was founded in 1947. Membership now numbers in the thousands. Each year, in July or August, the IJA sponsors a North American Festival attended by over 1,000 jugglers and drawing competitors from all over the world to compete for the top awards in juggling.

Shower pattern depicted in an 18th century French wood cut.

Open access to juggling began in the late 1970s, first with books and later with videos that gave everyone an opportunity to learn the skill. Now it is a rare physical education program that does not have at least some juggling component, and literally hundreds of juggling organizations have been formed all over North America, at colleges, universities, secondary schools, and even elementary schools, and many of them even sponsor local juggling festivals.

chapter

2

Scarf Juggling

Specially designed, colorful, lightweight nylon scarves provide big, slow targets that make the juggling pattern easier to learn. While some people are ball shy, nobody is scarf shy. With scarves, you have the luxury of seeing your hands when you toss and when you catch, and you can easily learn the basic patterns of the cascade, the reverse cascade, and columns without developing some of the bad habits that occur when you learn with balls first. Because you must juggle scarves in a flat plane in front of you, scarf juggling can help you avoid the biggest problems with beginning ball juggling: running forward and scooping inward. Scarves can be bought in most independent toy or magic stores or over the Internet on our Web site. Plastic bags from the produce department of the grocery store provide a serviceable substitute when you are first learning.

1 • Cascade With Three Scarves

To learn the basic cascade pattern, start with one scarf. Pinch the scarf in the center and let it hang down like a "ghost" (figure 2.1a). Raise your arm across your chest, toss with your palm out, and flick the scarf as high as it will go (figure 2.1b). Reach up high with your other hand and catch straight down. Claw like a lion to catch (figure 2.1c). Toss across in the other direction and claw down.

The scarf follows a figure eight or "infinity sign" path as shown in figure 2.1a. Say, "throw across, catch down, throw across, catch down" as you practice. Once this pattern is smooth, go on to the next step.

Figure 2.1 Basic infinity sign pattern: *(a)* start in the "ghost" position, *(b)* toss, and *(c)* claw down to catch.

Hold a scarf in each hand in the ghost position. Toss the first one across, as you did with one scarf (figure 2.2a). Throw from the shoulder and flick your wrist to toss as high as you can. When the first scarf gets to the top, look at it and throw the second scarf across in the opposite direction (figure 2.2b). The scarves make an X as they cross in front of your chest.

After you toss, both your hands should be high in the air with your palms out. Catch the scarf you threw first straight down (figure 2.2c), then catch the second one straight down with your other hand. Remember, the first one you throw is the first one you catch, but you catch it with your other hand. Say, "throw-throw-catch-catch" as you practice. The scarf that started out in your left hand ends up in your right, and vice versa. Cross to throw, come straight down to catch. Establish a nice even rhythm with pauses between the throws and equal pauses between the catches.

Figure 2.2   Crisscross with two scarves: *(a)* first toss, *(b)* second toss,

(continued)

Figure 2.2   *(continued) and (c) reach straight down to catch.*

If you have the habit of one hand throwing and the other hand simply passing across, you will find that it is the dominant hand that likes to throw and the nondominant hand that likes to pass across. To break this habit, start with the nondominant hand. Toss your two scarves slowly, one at a time, starting with your nondominant hand. If you are right-handed, as you do this, say, "Throw left, throw right, hands in the air." Then try "Throw left, throw right, hands in the air, catch right, catch left, hands come down." If you do this properly, you should be able to break the habit quickly.

Now on to continuous cascade juggling using three scarves! Hold two scarves in your dominant hand, with one deep in your hand and one held loosely on the fingertips. Hold one scarf in your nondominant hand. (See figure 2.3a.) The one on the fingertips in the dominant hand is the first scarf you throw. When #1 gets to the top, throw #2 from your other hand (figure 2.3b). As your hand comes straight down after throwing #2 across, it quickly catches #1. Then, when #2 gets to the top, throw #3. It goes to the same peak as #1 (figure 2.3c). As your hand comes down from throwing #3,

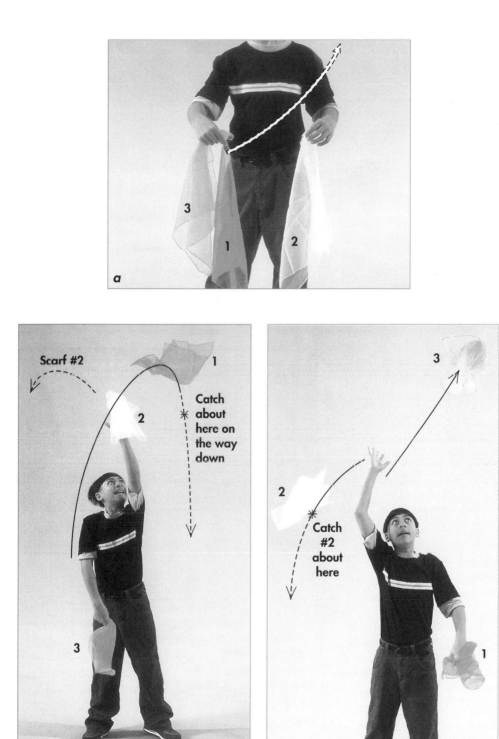

Figure 2.3 Cascade with three scarves: *(a)* starting position; *(b)* throwing #2 and getting ready to catch #1; *(c)* throwing #3 and getting ready to catch #2.

it quickly catches #2, and you throw #4 (which is #1 coming around again). Keep alternating your hands: right, left, right, left. Toss high and go slowly. All tosses are from the shoulder with your palm out, like waving goodbye. All catches are with the palm down, clawing like a lion.

Another way to think of the pattern is to realize that you have only one scarf in the air most of the time. As the one in the air begins to fall, you replace it by throwing from your other hand. Then, with that empty hand, instantly retrieve that first scarf in the air. As soon as either hand is empty, use it to quickly claw downward and catch the scarf already in the air. If you start with two scarves in your right hand, what you say while you juggle is: "Throw right, throw left and catch, throw right and catch, throw left and catch, throw right and catch."

Here are all the rules for continuous cascade juggling:

1. Start with the scarf on the fingertips in the hand that has two scarves in it.
2. Throw with your arms relatively straight, using your shoulders to toss as high as you can.
3. Flick your wrist at the last moment for added height.
4. Toss across your body forming an X and releasing as high as possible.
5. Focus on the peaks; notice each scarf when it gets to the top.
6. Every time one gets to the top, toss another, and with your empty hand catch the one that's in the air by clawing straight down.
7. Alternate your hands and count, "1-2-1-2," or say "right, left, right, left," or play music with a nice steady beat.
8. Go slowly. Scarf juggling is soft and flowing.

Have fun and teach others this simple cascade pattern. Put on music with different tempos and try to juggle the cascade pattern at different speeds, tossing to different heights. Don't be satisfied with just this one juggling pattern; there are many more. Keep practicing and keep learning.

2 • Columns

Columns are like elevator shafts. Each scarf goes up and comes down along its own pathway. The easiest way to learn columns is to learn two in one hand first. Start by kneeling tall behind two scarves that are lying on the ground side by side. Put one hand behind your back and hold onto your shirt or belt so that you won't be tempted to use that hand. Grab one scarf with your palm down, toss that one scarf high in the air, and let it fall to the ground. Now toss the other scarf high in the air in a pathway parallel to the first and let it fall to the ground. Toss one, toss the other, toss one, toss the other. Eventually you will build up your speed and start catching the scarves before they hit the ground. Once you can do this with one hand, try the other hand. Once you can do it in either hand, columns should be easy to learn.

Hold two scarves in one hand and one in the other. From the fingertips of the hand that has two scarves, throw the scarf straight up the center (figure 2.4a). When it gets to the top, throw the other two scarves at the same time straight up the sides (figure 2.4b). As your hands come down, catch the one scarf as shown in figure 2.4c, then immediately throw it again, straight up the middle. As your hands come down from throwing one, they catch the two and toss them straight up again. Now every scarf has its own pathway, like three elevator shafts. You can toss the one scarf up the middle with your right hand or with your left hand or with both hands. As you do this trick, say, "One up the middle and two up the sides, one up the middle and two up the sides."

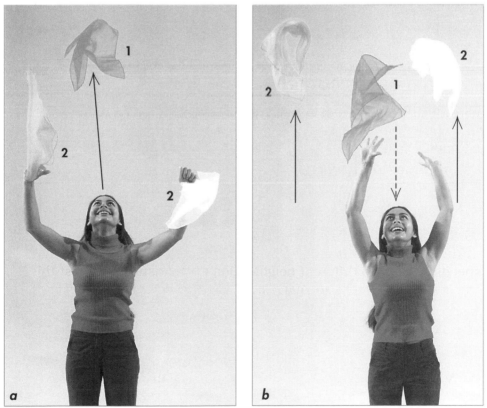

Figure 2.4 Columns: *(a)* throw one up the middle, *(b)* two up the sides,

(continued)

Figure 2.4   *(continued) and (c)* catch.

*W*hile doing columns, when one scarf is in the air, you can hold the other two and turn a pirouette. Then as soon as you get around, toss the two up the sides and catch the one. Another variation of columns is to toss the one scarf up one side and the two up the other side. This can be very humorous as you run frantically back and forth between the two scarves going up one side and the one scarf going up the other side, tossing them all as high as possible. Stay facing toward the audience while you dash back and forth.

3 ● *Reverse Cascade*

In the cascade you toss the scarves up out of the center of the infinity sign, release them over your far shoulder, and catch them as they go down the outside. In the reverse cascade you toss by bringing the scarves up the outside, releasing high over the near shoulder, and tossing them so that they fall down the center. The scarves are still following an infinity sign pathway, but everything is in reverse.

First, practice tossing one scarf along this pathway. The one scarf goes up the outside, over in an arc, and down the center, and your other arm comes down the center to catch. Now try two scarves, one in each hand. Toss the first one from the right hand by moving up the outside in an arc and release the scarf at a peak over the right shoulder so that it comes down the center. Then toss the second scarf from the left hand to a similar peak over the left shoulder. The left hand keeps coming down the center and catches the first scarf as soon as that hand is empty; meanwhile, the empty right hand circles over again and catches the second scarf. Pause and repeat. Learn to start with either the right or the left hand.

Now try three. Begin as you do in the cascade, with two scarves in your dominant hand and one in your nondominant hand. Start with the hand that has two and throw the first scarf with the big overhand throw you have been practicing (figure 2.5a). As it begins to fall down the center, toss the second scarf from the other hand with that same big overhand throw, and catch the first (figure 2.5b). Now just keep making big arm circles, and as the third scarf comes down, catch the second. Alternate your arms, right, left, right, left. All throws are from the outside and all catches are down the center.

Figure 2.5   Reverse cascade: *(a)* toss #1 with a big overhand throw,

(continued)

Figure 2.5   *(continued) and (b)* as it starts to descend, toss #2 and catch #1.

S*tart by visualizing an imaginary basketball hoop above your head and slightly in front. Pretend to turn double Dutch with two long jump ropes and with empty hands. Keep your arms straight and make big arm circles up the outside and down the center. Now try the same move with three scarves. Your job is to shoot baskets and turn double Dutch at the same time. The scarves go up the outside and down the center, and your arms make big circles.*

4 • *Under the Leg*

First just practice tossing one scarf under your leg. Let's start on the right. Raise your right leg, toss a scarf under it from your right hand by reaching deeply under your knee, catch the scarf with your left hand, and lower your leg. Now that you can toss a scarf under your leg and catch it in the other hand, the next step is to start juggling in the cascade pattern by tossing your first scarf under your right leg from your right hand. Start by holding two scarves in the right hand, raise your right leg and toss your first scarf under the leg, lower the leg quickly, and continue juggling in the cascade pattern. Next hold two scarves, one in each hand. Toss the left-hand scarf up from left to right, and as soon as it peaks, raise your right knee as high as you can and toss the right-hand scarf under your upraised knee. Catch the scarf that went over your leg in your right hand and the one that went under your leg in your left hand. Next try the trick in the middle of your three-scarf juggling pattern. As the scarf from your left hand peaks, raise your right knee, toss your scarf under the knee from your right hand, and quickly lower the knee. (See figure 2.6.)

Once you can toss under your right leg, learn to toss under your left leg. Then work on tossing every third scarf under a leg, alternating right and left. Learn to toss under the left leg from the right hand and under the right leg from the left hand. You need to reach across your body for this. One of your first and most impressive tricks can be a succession of throws: right hand under right leg, right hand under left leg, left hand under right leg, left hand under left leg.

Figure 2.6   Reach deeply under your knee to toss the scarf under your leg and into the cascade pattern.

5 • Behind the Back or Over the Shoulder

First learn to toss one scarf behind the back or over the far shoulder. You can reach way around and under your other arm, then flick your wrist and toss as far and as high as you can, or you can reach high up and toss behind your back and over your opposite shoulder. Once you feel comfortable with this throw, toss one scarf from your left hand, and as soon as it peaks, toss the other scarf from your right behind the back or over the shoulder. The two scarves change hands. Next, learn to start by tossing the first scarf over your shoulder or behind your back.

Now it's time to work the move into your routine. Start juggling normally, and just before you would normally toss your scarf from your right hand in the cascade pattern, bring your arm behind your back and toss #1 either under your other arm or over your opposite shoulder (figure 2.7). Quickly bring your right arm back around, catch the incoming scarf (#3) with your right hand, and continue to juggle without a pause. The scarf that was thrown from your right hand arrived at your left hand at exactly the same moment it would have if it had come along the normal route, so you don't need to break your rhythm. Once you can do this move on one side, learn it on the other. Then try a succession of over-the-shoulder or behind-the-back throws.

Figure 2.7 Dorothy has just tossed #1 over her shoulder. Next, she will catch #3, then toss #2.

6 • *Blow Up*

You can start juggling with your head tilted back and a scarf draped over your face. Blow the scarf on your face up into the air and use it as your first toss (figure 2.8). Then experiment with blowing the scarf in the air. Keep two scarves going by blowing them in turn. Catch a scarf on your face and blow it back up. This surprising move is guaranteed to get a laugh, especially from young children.

Figure 2.8   Try blowing the scarf up and using it as the first toss in your juggling pattern.

7 • *Kick Up*

Start with a scarf draped on your foot. Kick it up and make it the first toss in your juggling pattern (figure 2.9). Experiment with dropping the scarf and kicking it back into the pattern, so if you do drop in your routine, it can look like a trick that you wanted to perform. Another move is to kick the fallen scarf from foot to foot with a soccer dribble, then kick it back up into the pattern.

Figure 2.9   Kick the scarf up into your juggling pattern.

8 • *Three in One Hand*

This move is really difficult, and it requires fast reflexes. You start by alternating two scarves in one hand; then once you have built up a rhythm, throw a third scarf extra high from your other hand (figure 2.10). Now each one has its own pathway and you continually grab the lowest scarf. The cue to toss is not the same as it was when you were doing two in one hand. You can't wait until the previous scarf gets to the top to toss the next one, but you just throw as fast as you can. This looks very difficult as the three scarves really fill the air with juggling.

Figure 2.10   To throw three in one hand, continually grab the lowest scarf and throw it as fast as you can.

*H*old your other hand up in the air or behind your back while you do this *fast and impressive trick. That way it is apparent that you are using just one hand to juggle all three scarves. If you can, at the end of the routine catch all three scarves in your one hand and pretend to wipe your brow with them for a guaranteed applause point.*

9 • *Juggling Three With a Partner*

When you learn to juggle three scarves with a partner, you will see that interactive juggling can be a lot of fun! Each person does one half of the juggling pattern. One juggler starts with two scarves in the right hand, and the other juggler starts with one scarf in the left (figure 2.11a). Put your empty hands behind your backs and face each other. The person with two scarves starts, just as the hand with two scarves starts when one person juggles alone. That person throws #1 as shown in figure 2.11b. When #1 peaks, the other person tosses #2 and catches #1 with that same hand (figure 2.11c). Then, the first person tosses #3 and catches #2. All you have to remember is to alternate jugglers, just as you alternated hands when you juggled alone. Say, "I throw, you throw, I throw, you throw."

To avoid collisions, reach high to make the catch, then toss under the scarf that is in the air. Don't speed up. Wait until your partner's scarf begins to fall before you throw yours. Avoid the temptation to use both hands.

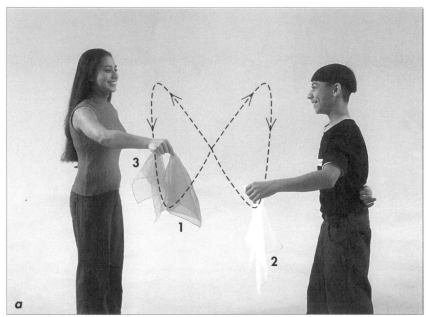

Figure 2.11 Juggling three with a partner: *(a)* starting position;

(continued)

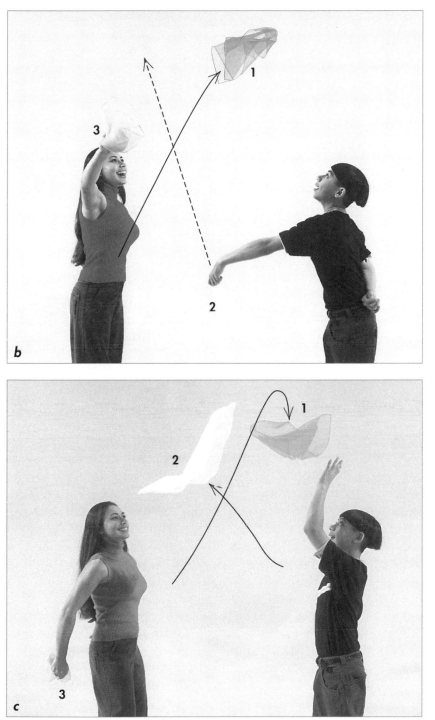

Figure 2.11 *(continued)* *(b)* Dorothy tosses #1; *(c)* Ben tosses #2 and catches #1 with that same hand.

Once you can toss three scarves back and forth while facing your partner, you can do this same pattern side by side, so you become a four-legged, two-headed, two-handed juggler. It is easier if you make contact with the other person. For instance, put your arms around each other's waists. The person with two scarves starts, and you just keep alternating, "me, you, me, you" (figure 2.12). For a laugh why not give your partner "bunny ears," or scratch his head, or take off his hat with your free hand, putting it on your own head.

Figure 2.12   Side by side juggling.

10 • *Passing Six With a Partner*

One person starts with four scarves, two in each hand. The other person starts with two, one in each hand. (See figure 2.13a.) The person with four scarves starts first and tosses two nice and high as if tossing over a volleyball net to the partner (figure 2.13b). Once the two scarves start to fall, the other person tosses two under the incoming scarves, but over that same volleyball net (figure 2.13c). Each partner can chant quietly (so as not to confuse the other), "You, me, you, me." To avoid collisions, scoop under the scarves in the air and toss nice and high. Aim at two points above your partner's shoulders. When you look at this pattern from the side, it is still a figure eight or infinity sign.

Avoid the natural tendency to back away from your partner. You should be about as far away as your arms can reach, around five or six feet at the most. To keep the pattern going as slowly as possible, wait until your partner's scarves are almost to you before throwing. Concentrate on making good throws with a high arc. If you make good throws, the catches will be easy.

Now that you can juggle three scarves, it is time to give your first show. Let others see your remarkable progress and invite them to learn. Because you have scarf juggling under control, you can learn almost any complex juggling move in slow motion with scarves before trying it with balls. If you keep three scarves in your pocket, you will never be bored, and certainly never boring, again.

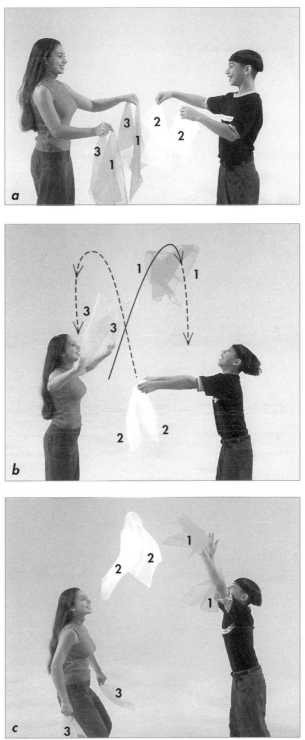

Figure 2.13 Passing six with a partner: (a) starting position; (b) Dorothy tosses two; (c) Ben tosses two and catches the incoming scarves.

chapter

3

Three-Ball Juggling

Now that you know the timing and the basic juggling patterns, you are ready for the next step: beanbag or ball juggling. The only change you will need to make is to turn your palms up. The best way to learn to juggle three balls is to start with spherical beanbags, which are about the size of tennis balls, soft and forgiving when they hit your hand, and about four ounces in weight. The best of these are JuggleBeanBalls by Jugglebug, soft plastic balls with plastic pellets inside. They are durable and washable and have a tacky surface that helps you catch. They come in sets of three different colors, making it easy to follow the path of each ball through the pattern.

We will call everything in this chapter a ball, even though we usually mean a beanbag. The only time bouncy balls are preferred by jugglers is when they are doing bounce tricks. If you are looking for a good bouncy juggling ball, try a set of three Professor Confidence balls from Jugglebug for about $20. If you want a great juggling ball with a very high bounce, look for silicone balls available from major prop makers, but be prepared to pay over $100 for three.

To avoid bad habits, it is vital to learn cascade juggling with three beanbags first, before you try other tricks, especially two in one hand. The worst of these habits is what we call "the disease," and sometimes we find a whole school that has caught it. A well-meaning teacher or student learns to keep two beanbags or balls going in one hand with a forward shoveling motion and teaches everyone else this simple trick. The objects go in an inward circle, toward the chest of the juggler. This can lead to a primitive three-ball juggle with every ball tossed to a single central point in front. The only way to avoid collisions is to either scoop inward or run forward. While it is true that the balls are being juggled, this move is a dead end! It is much harder to break this shoveling habit than it is to learn from scratch. Do not try two balls in one hand until you can juggle well with three in a cascade without running forward! The key to staying in one place, and the key to learning more than just one primitive trick, is to juggle in a flat plane in front of you with two peaks. This chapter will help you to establish that plane.

11 ● *Three-Ball Cascade*

The cascade is the most basic three-ball juggling pattern that you return to constantly while juggling. Start with one beanbag. Toss it from hand to hand in the infinity sign pattern, with your palms up, as shown in figure 3.1.

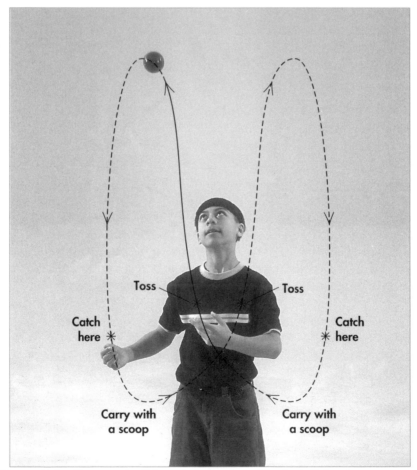

Figure 3.1   Toss one ball from hand to hand in the infinity sign pattern.

Imagine a microphone in front of you, at or above eye level, and toss under the microphone with every throw. Catch on the outside and scoop under the microphone again from the outside to the center. Catch the ball as if it were an egg, cushioning the catch. As you catch, your hand should be moving in a U shape from the outside toward the center. Do not recoil or cock your hand to toss again; just keep moving with this scooping toss.

This move must be very smooth and flowing with no pauses. At first your peaks should be high on each side, at least two feet above your shoulders. Do this over and over until it is a habit. Imagine a glass wall in front of you and keep the ball on this glass wall. Explore this flat wall. Move your peaks up and toss high and narrow for a few throws, then move your peaks down and out and toss low and wide, keeping the peaks on both sides at the same height. Once you can fill the flat imaginary windowpane in front of you with smooth infinity signs over and over again without pausing or recoiling your hand, it is time to move on to the next step.

Although this move may seem boring or trivial because it involves only one ball, defining the pathway that balls will follow is the most important step in establishing a good, consistent juggling pattern. If you skip this step or if you do not pay attention to the details implied in this step, you will end up with a sloppy pattern that will be very difficult to adjust later. Bad habits are easy to learn and difficult to unlearn.

Now, hold two balls, one in each hand, palms up. Toss one on the infinity sign pathway across your chest. When it peaks, above your shoulder on the opposite side, toss the second ball to the same height, but above the other shoulder. (See figure 3.2.) The two balls make an X across your

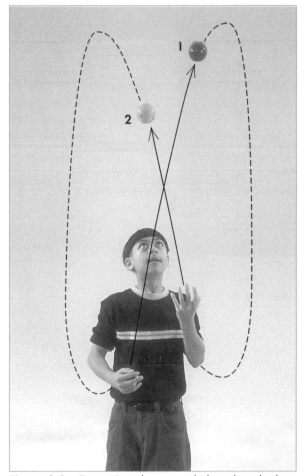

Figure 3.2   Toss #1 with your right hand and when it peaks, toss #2 to the same height on the opposite side.

chest. If you have any problems with this move, such as passing across instead of tossing the second ball, or throwing both at the same time, start with your nondominant hand. Since it is the one that usually needs help, make it the leader. Remember the imaginary glass wall in front of you and keep your juggling pattern flat, on that wall. Don't shovel in toward yourself, just scoop under the imaginary microphone from the outside toward the center. At the moment you see the first ball hit the peak and begin to fall, toss with a scoop in the other direction.

Because your throws are more important than your catches, practice two good throws (to the same height) without any catches. Next, work on your catches. Be careful not to reach up to catch; when you catch, your hands should be at about the same height that they were when you threw.

Once you can toss and catch two balls in an X 10 times without dropping, it is time to move on to three. Start with two in one hand; the first ball is on your fingertips in the hand that holds two, and the second one is held comfortably in your other hand. The third ball is on the heel of the hand behind number one. (See figure 3.3a.) Juggling three is simply repeating the move you just learned over and over, without stopping.

Start with the hand that has two. Look up at the peaks. Make Xs with your throws. Alternate your hands. Every time one gets to the peak, toss another, under the imaginary microphone, across and up to the peak on the other side. In figure 3.3b Ben has tossed #1, then as it peaked he threw #2. In figure 3.3c, #1 has been caught and #2 is just at the peak, so he now tosses #3 to the same peak as #1.

Your job is to always have one ball in the air; as it begins to fall, you toss another one. You should never have two in your hand again. If you see you are going to have two, toss the one that is in that hand so that you can catch with an empty hand.

Remember that wall in front of you. Don't throw forward or you will walk forward. Toss to the same height on both sides. Don't reach up to catch. Let the balls come down to you and catch them softly as though they were eggs. Alternate your hands and count cadence as you juggle: "right, left, right, left." When you want to stop, stop cleanly by catching the last ball on a fingertip nest formed by your thumb and first two fingers. The ball that is already in your hand is rolled back and held by your ring finger and pinkie.

At first you will juggle high in the air, but with practice you can juggle smaller and smaller. Eventually the pattern will be down below your eyes, and you can look at the audience, just noticing the peaks with your peripheral vision. That's cool!

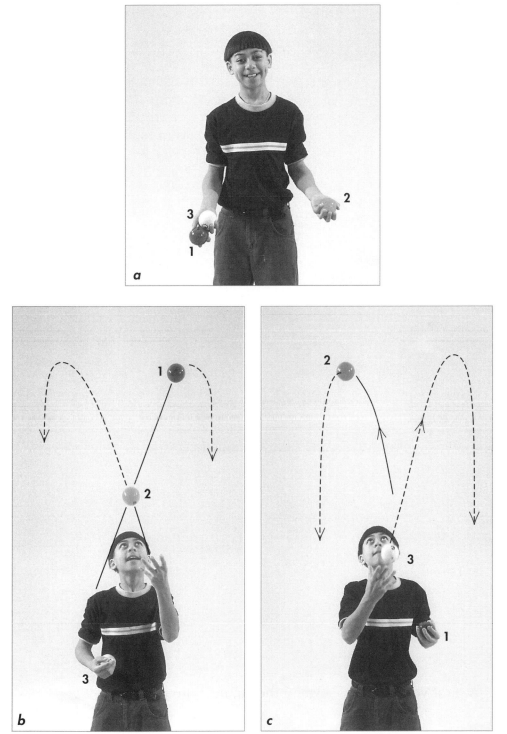

Figure 3.3 Cascade with three balls: *(a)* Ball #1 will be thrown first; *(b)* as #1 peaks, throw #2 and catch #1; *(c)* as #2 peaks, throw #3.

Common Problems and Solutions

1. "My third ball goes out in front!"

   Solution—Your first throw and your third throw must be identical. Once #1 has left your fingertips, roll #3 forward to the same position, and when #2 peaks, toss #3 to the same spot as #1, with the same scoop. Make certain that all throws from your problem hand feel the same. Remember, there are only two throws, a right-hand throw and a left-hand throw, and they are symmetrical to identical peaks over each shoulder. As you juggle, say, "one, two, one, two," or "right, left, right, left." Put on music with a good beat, such as swing or old-time rock and roll, and juggle to the beat. You can bob your knees up and down, but don't walk forward.

2. "I go for three or four throws and then I drop!"

   Solution—You need to notice your peaks and make certain you are hitting the same height on each toss, not going lower and lower. Also, make sure you do not reach up higher and higher every time you catch. The time the ball is in the air is determined by the height of your toss and the height at which you catch. To establish a rhythm, this distance should be the same every time.

3. "My balls collide!"

   Solution—Exaggerate those side-to-side scoops and make certain you are juggling in a flat plane in front of you, not shoveling in from the front. Collisions can also be caused by rushing. Toss higher and wider and go more slowly. Get the beat! Juggling is a rhythm instrument!

Although we say, "a drop is a sign of progress" and, "you learn to juggle drop by drop," don't repeat the same mistake over and over. Stop, analyze the problem, and make adjustments using the information in this chapter. The objective is to be able to keep juggling without stopping or dropping.

12 • *Reverse Cascade*

Doing the reverse cascade with balls is just like doing it with scarves except that your palms are up. Imagine that you have a basket in front of you, just above your head. Begin by establishing the pathway with one ball (figure 3.4). Toss it in a short arc that goes from the outside and down the center, through the basket. That imaginary basket is your target. Then catch in the center with the other hand and toss from that hand. Say, "Toss over and catch, toss over and catch."

Figure 3.4 Toss one ball in the reverse cascade pathway.

Once this pathway is familiar and you are comfortable with this new way of making an infinity sign with one ball, try two balls—two throws and two catches. Start with one ball in each hand. Toss your first ball into the imaginary basket. Then toss over from the opposite hand. Catch both balls and pause. Try it again and again until it is easy to do. Say, "Over, over, catch, catch."

Now hold two balls in one hand and one in the other. Start with the hand that has two and keep throwing over. It will feel awkward at first, but just keep saying "over, over, over, over," until you have developed this new habit. You should have two distinct peaks very close to the center. Every ball goes into the basket, and every one follows the same path. See figure 3.5.

As with the cascade, you should practice as though you have a glass wall in front of you. Fill this wall with the reverse cascade pattern. Juggle in a big high pattern to start, and then gradually bring your basket down until you can juggle very fast and very small. Then try wider and wider, and higher and higher. Your goal is to gain complete mastery of every pathway that a ball could take on the flat plane in front of you.

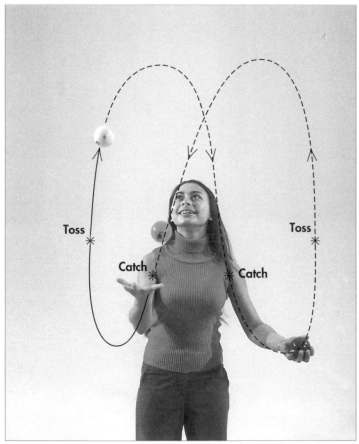

Figure 3.5   Reverse cascade: Catch on the inside, and scoop and toss from the outside.

13 • *Half Shower and Jugglers' Tennis*

Now that you can juggle with throws that come up the center and go down the outside (cascade) and throws that go up the outside and down the center (reverse cascade), you can combine these two moves and immediately get three new tricks. You can toss over with all your right-hand throws and under with all your left-hand throws; this is called a half shower from the right (figure 3.6). When you toss over with all throws from the left and under with all throws from the right, this is called a half shower from the left.

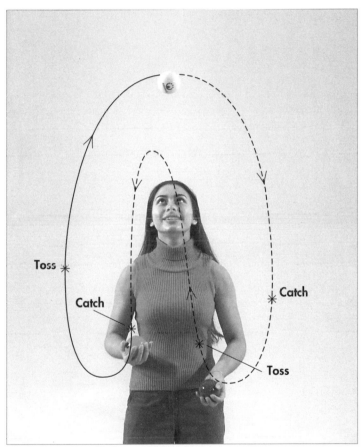

Figure 3.6   Half shower from the right.

Finally, you can identify one odd ball and toss this ball back and forth over the top of the pattern with a very wide reverse cascade throw while you juggle two balls underneath in the smaller cascade pattern (figure 3.7). The order in which you throw the balls is the same, but every time the odd ball (#3) comes down, reach out, grab it, and throw it higher and farther than the other two, so it goes up the outside and over your entire pattern. You can pause a bit before tossing the ball from the hand that the odd ball is going to, then toss the odd ball back immediately when it gets to that hand, also in a big, high arc. The odd ball going over the top looks like a tennis ball going over a net. You can shoot lobs and smashes with this odd ball, and even run back and forth as it zooms far out over the pattern. This is called jugglers' tennis.

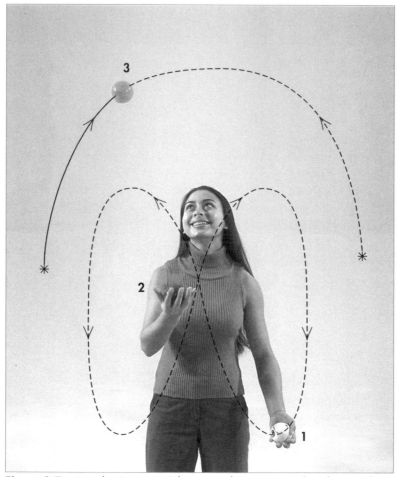

Figure 3.7   Jugglers' tennis. (The asterisks represent the places where you catch and throw ball #3.)

14 • *Two in One Hand and Columns*

Before you try this trick, make sure you can juggle three in a flat plane. Otherwise, you may develop the very bad habit of shoveling in toward yourself, a habit that will take a great deal of effort to break.

Start with two balls in one hand. Toss the one on your fingertips straight up the center. When it gets to the top, move your hand to the outside and toss the other one straight up in a parallel pathway (figure 3.8). Your hand shifts back and forth while the two balls go straight up and down. Next, learn to toss the balls in a circle that goes from the center toward the outside (as shown in figure 3.9), and in a circle that goes from the outside toward the center. These three patterns—columns, outside circles, and inside circles—are the only ways you can juggle two in one hand and keep the pattern in a flat plane in front of you. The balls travel on that imaginary wall. Don't shovel in toward yourself. Work with just two dimensions, height and width, but not depth.

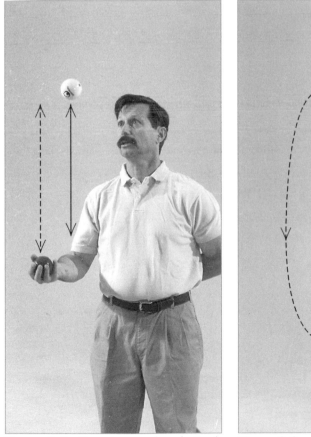

Figure 3.8 Two in one hand. Each ball has its own parallel pathway.

Figure 3.9 Outside circles.

Once you can do two balls in each hand, it is time to learn columns with three. Start by tossing the first ball, the one on your fingertip nest, straight up the center (figure 3.10a). As soon as it peaks, toss two balls up the sides at the same time (figure 3.10b). You can catch the one ball in either hand or even in both hands. Toss it immediately straight up the middle again, and catch and toss the two outside balls at the same time. Then just keep one ball going up and down in the middle and two going up and down on the sides.

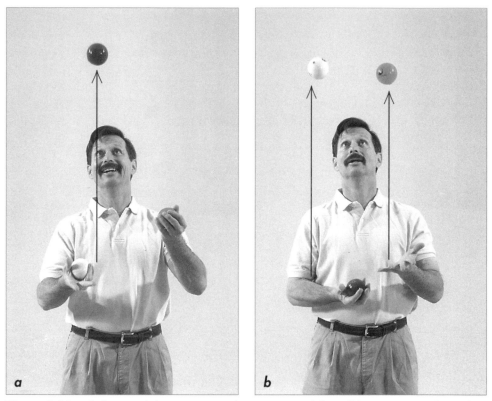

Figure 3.10 Columns: *(a)* toss one up the center and then *(b)* toss two up the sides.

*N*ow *that you are developing a repertoire, it is time to learn to make smooth transitions between your various juggling moves. Start with columns, and while you have one ball in the air, cross under with one of the others and go into the cascade without stopping. Stay in the cascade for a while, and then toss one up the middle instead of going across to the other hand, and you will go back into columns. Now try to go from cascade to reverse cascade. The easiest way is to say "under, under, under" as you do the cascade, and shift to saying "over, over, over" as you do the reverse. If you have learned to juggle with scarves, try your transitions first with them. This will make the transitions with balls far easier.*

15 • Yo-Yo

To learn the popular "yo-yo," practice juggling two balls in your dominant hand in side-by-side columns. Then bring your other hand up and just hold that empty hand where you can see it while continuing to juggle the two balls in your dominant hand. The objective is to just get used to seeing that other hand without getting "spooked" by it. While continuously juggling two in your dominant hand, experiment with moving your nondominant hand, randomly at first, and then parallel to one of the balls in your dominant hand.

Once this feels comfortable, it is time to hold a ball in your nondominant hand. You can hold the held ball

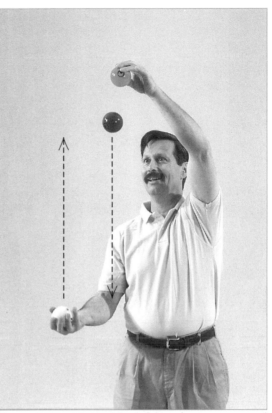

Figure 3.11 Yo-Yo: The left hand moves up and down as if linked to the ball in the air.

above the ball that is being tracked, a trick called the "yo-yo" (figure 3.11), or hold it below, which is called the "oy-oy." You can even move the held ball in circles around the ball in the air, "around the world," or in circles around your head, "the halo." As with all asymmetrical moves it is important to learn these variations with both your dominant and nondominant hands.

Figure 3.12   Keep your palms down while clawing.

16 ◦ *Clawing*

Clawing is like scarf juggling: you catch with the palm down and toss with the palm out. Start with one ball and toss it from hand to hand with your palms down, following the infinity sign path. Then try two and then three. (See figure 3.12.) Just follow that infinity sign path. Start higher and slower at first, then claw smaller and faster until the balls are down below your eyes. A fast, low claw is great training for fast and accurate juggling, and the audience loves it. You might call it "the tax collector" when you perform the move.

Once you can claw the balls every time, try to claw occasionally while juggling in the cascade pattern. Eventually you should be able to catch either way with any ball, with your palm up or with your palm down. Clawing can be very dynamic and surprising to the audience. It is an essential building block in many of the more complex juggling tricks that require you to move a ball quickly through your pattern.

17   *Shower*

In many parts of the world this speedy circular pattern is all there is to juggling. The dominant hand does all the throwing and the nondominant hand does all the catching. The catching hand just passes every ball quickly across to the throwing hand. Because the shower pattern reinforces the dominant hand and puts the other hand in the subordinate position of passing across, if you learn this pattern first, you will have trouble learning the many symmetrical patterns in which both hands must toss and both must catch.

To learn, start with two balls in your dominant hand and nothing in your nondominant hand. Throw the two balls one at a time in a high arc so rapidly that the second ball is well on its way when the first one lands. All catching is done in your nondominant hand with the palm up. Just say, "throw, throw, catch, catch."

Now put ball #3 in your nondominant hand. Throw the two from your dominant hand in rapid succession and to exactly the same height, just as you did a moment ago. Before you catch #1, pass #3 across to your dominant hand with a very short toss and catch both of the thrown balls in your nondominant hand in the order you threw them. (See figure 3.13.) Say, "throw, throw, pass, catch, catch."

To keep going, just keep throwing. Every time a ball comes to your dominant hand, throw it immediately along the high arc you have created, and to exactly the same height. Every time you catch a ball in your nondominant had, pass it quickly across to the dominant one. Consistency is the key. All your throws must be to the same height. Just say, "throw, throw, pass and throw, pass and throw, pass and throw, pass and throw." The pattern eventually becomes automatic.

Certainly it is exciting when you learn the shower pattern from your dominant hand. However, in order to prevent becoming too dependent on your dominant hand, it is very important to go through these same steps in the opposite direction and learn to toss with your nondominant hand and catch with the dominant one.

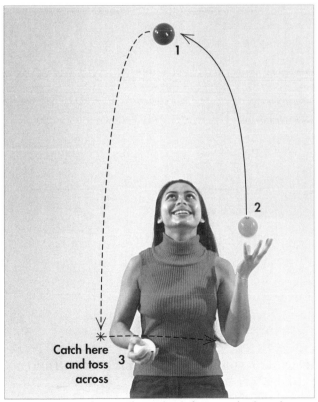

Figure 3.13 Shower from the left. Dorothy has thrown two balls from her left hand and is about to pass the third ball across from right to left.

18 ● Seesaw

Once you can do the shower both ways, you can do it a few times in one direction and go directly to a few times in the other direction, back and forth. My personal favorite is three times shower to the right, three times shower to the left, twice shower to the right, twice shower to the left, then alternating once shower to the right and once shower to the left, back and forth about 10 times. In this last step of the "seesaw," there are two balls going straight up and down while the third ball goes straight across from hand to hand, as shown in figure 3.14. This "seesaw" is very difficult, but worth the work.

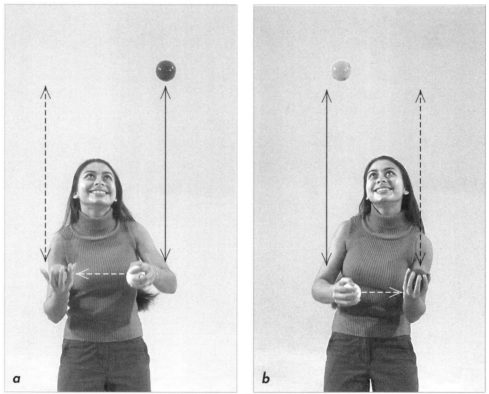

Figure 3.14   Seesaw: *(a)* to the left and *(b)* to the right.

19 • *Under the Leg*

To learn to do any trick in the middle of your routine, always learn to do the trick with a single ball first. Then you can try it as a start to your juggling pattern, and then in the middle of the routine. For instance, if you are trying to toss balls under each of your legs in turn, start with one ball and toss it back and forth under one leg and then under the other. Raise your knee very high to toss under so that you don't have to change your normal pattern much. Remember that there are four variations: tossing with the right hand under the right leg and under the left leg, and tossing with the left hand under the left leg and under the right leg.

Once you can do this smoothly, learn to start your routine by tossing your first ball under either leg with either hand and going straight into your routine.

To do the move under the right leg with the right hand in the middle of the pattern, start juggling and just after you toss with your left hand, quickly raise your right knee high, toss under it (as shown in figure 3.15), and quickly lower the leg again. The pattern doesn't change. The leg needs to go up high enough and fast enough to make the toss under the knee, and it needs to be back down again before the next throw. If you have one ball that is different from the other two, you can say to yourself, "When the red ball comes to my right hand, I am going to toss it under my right leg." Use a verbal cue such as "red under right" to remind yourself. Try the same with the red ball and your left leg. Then try the red ball under each leg in turn. Give yourself a cue such as, "Red under right, red under left, red under right, red under left." You can use this same breakdown of steps to learn any complex move. Remember to invent your own reminder words so that you verbally reinforce your tosses.

Figure 3.15   Raise your knee high to toss under your leg.

*E*ventually, if you are in shape, you can simply keep tossing alternately under both legs with every throw. Continuous tosses under both legs means you need to jog quickly in place, raising your knees as high as you can. This is a very fast aerobic workout that will definitely give you abs of steel. Tell your audience you are "juggling the hard way." They'll get the point.

20 • Over the Shoulder

Now you will be breaking out of the flat plane you have so carefully established and working in three dimensions, which makes learning more difficult and can lead to drops and frustration. Just remember that every new pattern you learn is a new set of habits that you need to imprint on your body and in your mind. Remember the practice it took to learn the cascade, and be persistent. You can learn these moves, but it will take time. In general it takes about one hour of concentrated work to learn a new three-ball trick, but it may take many hours of practice to perfect it enough to fit it into your routine.

To learn to toss behind your back and over your far shoulder, start with one ball and learn the pathway. Toss behind your back with your right hand, catch in front with the left, then toss behind the back with your left hand and catch in front with the right. Reach up high to throw. Learn to look up and to the right or to the left and just notice the peaks.

Next, holding one ball in each hand, toss one up and over the far shoulder. When you see it peak, toss the ball from your other hand in the usual cascade pattern across your chest. Catch them in the same order you threw them. Pause and try again.

Starting with two balls in your dominant hand, toss the fingertip ball, #1, over your far shoulder to start, pause until you see it peak, then toss the ball in your nondominant hand into the cascade pattern. Bring the hand out from behind your back, and you should now be juggling.

Now try the same move while juggling continuously. We'll describe the learning process for a right-handed person; simply reverse the process if you are left-handed. Concentrate on one marked ball that you can identify. Start juggling in the cascade pattern. Immediately after that marked ball comes to your right hand, reach quickly behind your back to throw up and across so that it goes over your left shoulder. Quickly bring your right hand back out in front so that you are prepared to catch the previously thrown ball that will soon be coming to that hand. Look up and to the left. The ball you just tossed behind your back comes into view over your left shoulder, and you toss the ball that is in your left hand just as you see the marked ball appear over your left shoulder. At this point you should be juggling in the cascade pattern again.

The over the shoulder toss is shown in figure 3.16 where Ben has tossed ball #3 over his far shoulder. Now he must quickly reach back out in front with his right hand to catch #2. Then he will toss #1 before catching #3.

The secret to continuous tosses behind the back with one hand is not to rush your throws and break the rhythm. Just toss every ball that comes to your right hand behind the back in the same tempo and to the same height as your tosses in front. That means tossing every throw from each hand a bit higher, not just the tosses behind your back. Keep that tempo, and every time a ball comes to your right hand, instead of tossing it across your chest, toss it across behind your back. You reach out front to catch and behind to throw. Practice with each hand in turn.

Figure 3.16 Tossing over the shoulder.

21 • Back Crosses

You can eventually send every toss from behind the back so that all catches are in front and all tosses are over the opposite shoulder. Start with two throws in succession, and as you toss, say, "right over, left over," then continue to juggle. Next do three throws and say, "right over, left over, right over," and continue to juggle. Keep adding one more toss each time, and remind yourself with your verbal cue. Eventually, you can cut out the cues and toss continual back crosses.

The back cross is shown in figure 3.17. When ball #1 peaked, Dorothy tossed #2 behind her back and is about to reach out and catch #1 (figure 3.17a). In figure 3.17b she has caught #1; ball #2 has just passed the peak, and she is tossing #3. Next she'll reach out and catch #2, then toss #1.

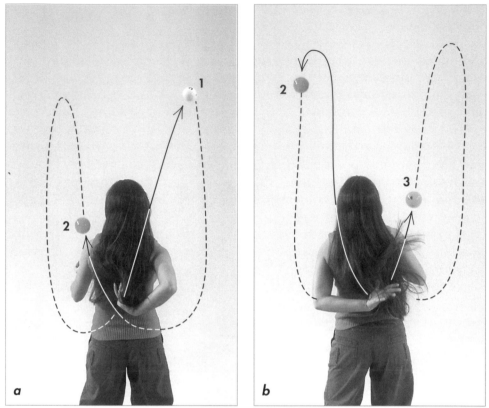

Figure 3.17   Tossing continual back crosses: *(a)* to the left and *(b)* to the right.

Here are a few pointers for successful back crosses:

- Practice with empty hands, turn your head from side to side, move your arms, but don't throw.
- Reach high to throw and practice with one ball throwing over each shoulder in turn.
- Practice with two balls and toss over each shoulder in turn.
- Practice starting to juggle with the first toss over your shoulder.
- Toss higher than usual to give yourself more time, but gradually reduce the height of every toss.
- Your catches are all in front, but blind, as your head is turned the opposite way when you catch.
- Your throws are all from the back and must be precise to make catching easier.

22 • *Pauses*

Pauses in your routine will add drama and comic relief to your performances. Pause for applause or to accent your performance. It helps if your pause comes as a "shock" in the midst of furious juggling. The audience builds up tension as you get creative and take more risks. They need to release this tension, so you pause, look at them, wink or smile, and resume the activity. Places to catch a beanbag for a surprising pause include the top of the foot, the forearm, the shoulder, the back of your hand, or the back of your neck. First learn the catch with a solo ball, then try it out of the pattern. Either catch the ball at the peak, when it isn't moving at all, or imagine that your ball is an egg and give way under it as you catch, absorbing the "shock" of the descending ball.

For the neck catch, don't toss high. Toss to normal height, but straight up. Look up until the last moment (figure 3.18a), then duck under with your arms forward and outstretched, in a "racing dive" position (figure 3.18b). Keep your head up and look at the audience. They will applaud at this automatic bow.

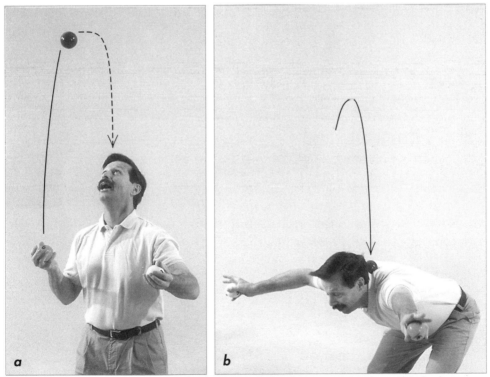

Figure 3.18   Neck catch: *(a)* look up until the last moment then *(b)* duck into a "racing dive" position.

Figure 3.19 Kick-up recovery.

23 ⦿ Recoveries

When you drop, you need a recovery that says, "I really meant to do that!" Don't just bend over and pick up the object. One fancy move is to clamp the ball between your heels, jump and kick to one side, bringing the ball over that same shoulder (figure 3.19). When you see that ball begin to fall from the peak, toss the ball from the hand that it is coming toward, and you are back in your pattern.

You can also roll the ball onto one foot using the other and kick it up in front, or while continuously juggling you can just bring your foot straight up to deliver the ball to your hand.

Another fun recovery is to simply drop the other two balls, fall to your knees, and make a "shell game" out of the three, hopping them over one another. Then stand up and start juggling again.

24 ⦿ Fancy Starts

A simple start that looks fancy is to hold two balls with your palm down, then with a twist of your wrist turn your palm up and let go. Balls 1 and 2 split and go in two different directions (figure 3.20). Toss ball #3 from your other hand up through this split. Catch the two balls at the same time and immediately toss the one from the hand that the solo ball is coming toward. Toss it under the one in the air, and you are automatically in the cascade.

Even fancier is to hold all three balls in your dominant hand and let your arm hang down. Quickly rotate your wrist so that your fingers are pointed up and toss all three at once. The center ball is held more loosely and goes higher than the others (figure 3.21). When the two outer balls are at their peaks, reach up and claw down on them while the center ball continues to climb. As the center ball starts to fall, toss the right-hand ball up and across in a cascade pattern. Now you are juggling.

You can also make this trick look a lot more difficult by tossing the group of three balls under your leg, or behind your back and over your opposite shoulder. The rules are still the same: claw the two lower balls downward and toss one under to get into the cascade pattern.

Figure 3.20 Simple split.

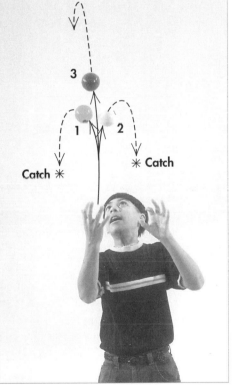

Figure 3.21 Toss three and claw down.

25 • Carries

By now you should have an impressive routine with plenty of tricks, applause points, and ways to start with flair and stop cleanly. The carry is one more tool that you can use to become a more "complete" juggler. Instead of tossing a ball to a particular point, you can carry it there and either drop it, pass it, or throw it to the other hand. For instance, you can carry the ball under your opposite arm and toss it straight up into the pattern (figure 3.22). The carry-under and the short toss straight up should take the same amount of time as the usual toss across your chest. Right after you carry and toss, the carrying hand needs to go back quickly to the "normal" position for the next catch.

You can also carry the ball to your head and let it drop off the side of your head and into the pattern. In figure 3.23 Dorothy has set #2 on her head with her right hand, and is about to catch #3. When #2 falls, she'll toss #1 up and across, and catch #2 in her left hand.

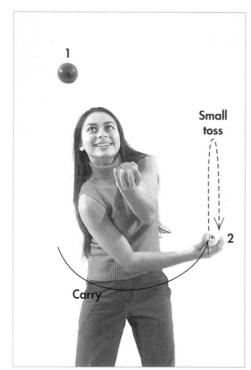

Figure 3.22 Carry under and toss up.

Figure 3.23 Carry to the head and let drop.

26 ● *Statue of Liberty*

Create the Statue of Liberty by throwing up to your extended arm and letting the balls drop down at a slight angle toward the throwing hand to be caught and thrown again. Leave your catching hand in the air with the arm extended (figure 3.24).

You learn the Statue of Liberty the way you learned the shower. Start with two in your left hand with your right hand held high. Throw the two balls quickly one after the other. After you have thrown them both, drop the ball out of your right hand. Now every time a ball comes to the right hand, drop it immediately, and every time a ball comes to the left hand, throw it.

Figure 3.24 To do the Statue of Liberty, leave your catching hand extended in the air.

27 • *Under the Arm*

This move is like jugglers' tennis except that your odd ball goes under the net, not over. You can use the carry you just learned, on both sides. Start with two balls, one in each hand. Cross your hands, right under left, toss the right-hand ball straight up, and follow immediately with a left-hand throw in the cascade pattern. Uncross your hands and catch the ball you threw from the right in the left hand, and the ball you threw from the left in the right hand.

Now, hold two balls in your right hand and one in the left. Cross your right hand under your left arm, toss the first ball straight up and the second in the cascade (figure 3.25), just as you did in the last step, then uncross your arms. As the second ball peaks, toss the third into the cascade pattern and start juggling.

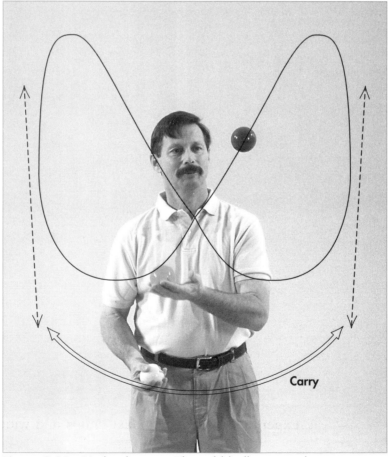

Figure 3.25 Under the arm: The odd ball goes under every time, while the other two balls follow the cascade pathway.

Next, learn this same series on the opposite side, crossing your left hand under your right.

Now you should be able to play "upside-down tennis." The odd ball is carried under from right to left, thrown straight up, and caught in the left hand; then it is carried under by that hand, thrown straight up on the opposite side, and caught in the right hand. This odd ball makes a U under the pattern, while the other two dance above in a cascade pattern.

28 • *Chops*

An especially challenging and athletic move that depends on carrying balls quickly through your pattern is the chop. Start with one ball in each hand. Carry the ball in your right hand up and back down in a big arc toward your left hand. As your right hand chops down toward this new position, toss the ball from your left hand under the wrist of the descending hand (figure 3.26), then toss the ball from your right hand in a short throw toward the left. The balls have crossed because you carried the ball across in your right hand. Separate your hands and catch.

Figure 3.26 Chop across with the right hand and toss straight up with the left.

Now try the move once while continuously juggling in the cascade pattern. Chop with the right hand in a big arc, toss the ball from the left hand, crossing under the wrist of the right hand and into the cascade pattern, then throw right, left, right, left, and keep juggling. Now try the move continuously with your right hand. Every time you catch with the right hand, chop across while you throw with the left under the right wrist. Then toss that small right-hand throw, move your right hand back to catch the next ball (the one that was thrown by your left hand under the right wrist), and repeat. Experiment with small, fast chops and wider, more dramatic chops.

Now learn this same series from the other side. Once you can chop on each side, learn to do two chops on both sides in succession. Every ball that crosses your chest is chopped, and every throw is straight up, under the opposite wrist.

In figure 3.27a Dorothy tossed #1 from her left hand under her right wrist, while chopping across in an arc from right to left with ball #2. In 3.27b, #2 was thrown from the right hand under the left wrist as #3 was chopped across.

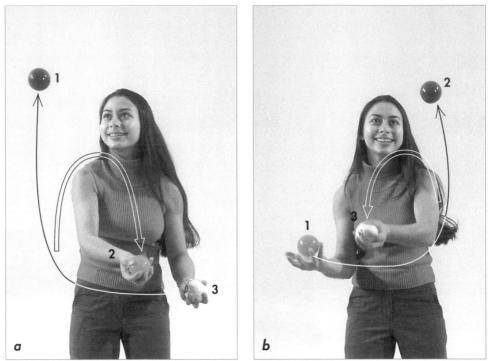

Figure 3.27 Chops *(a)* to the left and *(b)* to the right.

29 • *Mills' Mess*

Mills' Mess, created by Steve Mills, is a particularly complicated and challenging pattern that is well worth learning because it opens the door to many other tricks. There are many different ways to learn this pattern. We will explain our favorite. Two moves that are useful to know before you start are jugglers' tennis (page 35) and the Under the Arm (page 52). In Mills' Mess each ball follows its own path, so we will name our three balls blue (#1), red (#2), and yellow (#3). The blue and red balls appear to chase each other on the inside of the pattern each in their own variation of the cascade, while the yellow ball brackets the bottom and the sides of the pattern on a U-shaped pathway, just as it did in Under the Arm. Your arms cross right over left and then left over right as you execute the pattern.

Start with the blue ball, #1. Cross your arms. Hold the ball in the hand that is on top. Toss in an arc toward the center (figure 3.28a) while you uncross and recross your arms, putting the opposite arm on top so you can catch the ball (figure 3.28b). Catch just past the center in your opposite hand and continue carrying the ball in the direction that it is falling, bringing it to the outside of the pattern and putting it in position to repeat the move from the opposite side. Remember to establish two distinct peaks. Practice until it is a smooth reverse cascade pattern.

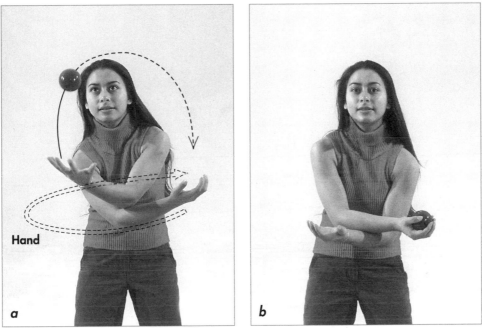

Figure 3.28   Mills' Mess: Pathway of the first ball.

Now it is time for the red ball, #2. Cross your arms and hold the ball in the hand that is on the bottom. Uncross your arms, and at the moment just before they are uncrossed, toss the red ball toward the center in a reverse cascade pattern (figure 3.29a). Recross your arms with the opposite one on top and catch the red ball in the hand that is underneath (figure 3.29b). Repeat the move from the opposite side. Practice until you see a distinct cascade with two peaks.

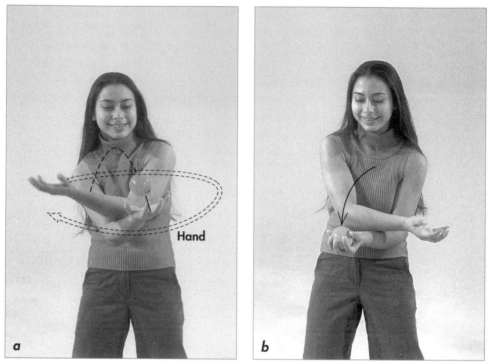

Hand

Figure 3.29   Mills' Mess: Pathway of the second ball.

Now it is time for the yellow ball, #3. Start with your arms uncrossed. Carry the ball under the opposite arm and throw straight up the side (figure 3.30). Uncross and let the ball fall straight down into the opposite hand. Practice from both sides until the move is smooth and you can see a distinct U-shaped pattern.

Now it is time to learn to manipulate the two inside balls, the blue (#1) and the red (#2). Hold the blue ball on top with your arms crossed. Now toss it toward the center following the reverse cascade pathway we practiced in the previous step. As soon as you throw the blue ball, begin to uncross your arms, and at the moment before they uncross, release the red ball back toward the center along its pathway. The red ball appears to follow the blue. Remember to recross your arms to catch (figure 3.31). The blue ball lands in the hand that is now on top and the red ball in the hand that is on the bottom. Now you are in position to repeat from the opposite side. As you practice this move, continually soften your catches so that the balls each follow their own distinct reverse cascade pathway and your arms continually uncross and recross.

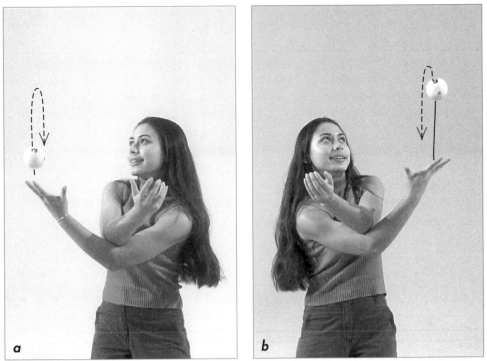

Figure 3.30 Mills' Mess: Pathway of the third ball.

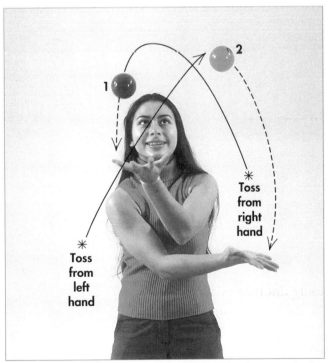

Figure 3.31 Mills' Mess: Combining the first two balls.

57

Now we put all these pieces together. In one hand, put the blue ball (#1) on your fingertips and the yellow ball (#3) on the heel of your hand. Put the red ball (#2) by itself in the other hand. Cross your arms with the hand that has two balls on top (figure 3.32a). Toss the blue ball toward the center, uncross your arms, and toss the red ball toward the center so that it is traveling in the same direction as the blue ball. Recross so that the blue ball lands in the opposite hand, the one that is now on top (figure 3.32b). As the red ball falls toward the hand holding the yellow ball, toss the yellow ball straight up and catch the red ball in that hand. Toss the blue ball toward the center again. Uncross your arms, and as you do, throw the red ball in the same direction as the blue. Recross your arms, carrying the yellow ball underneath the pattern. Toss the yellow ball straight up on the other side now, catch the red ball in that same hand, toss the blue, uncross, toss the red, cross, catch the blue with crossed arms, toss the yellow. Each ball now goes in its order and along its unique path. Count yourself forward, "blue, red, yellow, blue, red, yellow." (Hint: Don't try to figure this out; just follow the directions.)

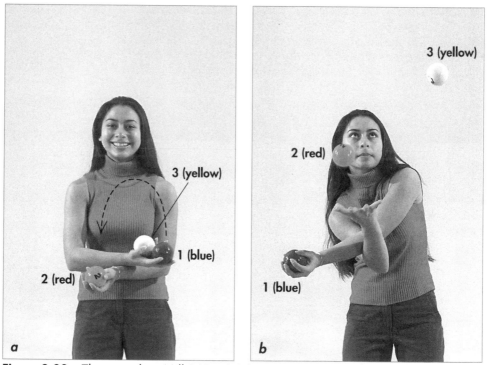

Figure 3.32 The complete Mills' Mess! *(a)* starting position; *(b)* Dorothy has tossed #1, uncrossed her arms, tossed #2, recrossed her arms, caught #1 and tossed #3, and is about to catch #2.

30 ● Body Bounces

Just think of all the parts of your body where a ball can be bounced. Toss one ball to that spot, bounce it, and catch it. Then hold three, bounce your first one off that spot, and start juggling. Finally, toss the ball out of a continuous juggle, bounce, and when it peaks, toss again, and you should be back in a juggle. Bounce off your forehead, knee, toe, instep, forearm (figure 3.33), elbow, or the back of your hand.

Figure 3.33   Bouncing off the forearm.

31 ● Floor Bounces

Now we switch from bounceless JuggleBeanBalls to bouncy rubber balls. Imagine a letter V from your hands to a spot on the ground just in front of you and in the center. Start with one ball and bounce it back and forth from hand to hand. Once you can do this successfully, throw one ball down (figure 3.34); as soon as it hits the ground, throw the second ball so that it goes to the outside of the V. When you bounce three balls, remember the letter V, start with the hand that has two, and go outside the V with every throw. The balls go down the outside and up the center.

Once you can juggle on the floor, experiment with all your different patterns—reverse cascade, two in one hand, and columns—by tossing down instead of up. Work on putting your leg through the cascade bouncing pattern so that one ball goes under your leg.

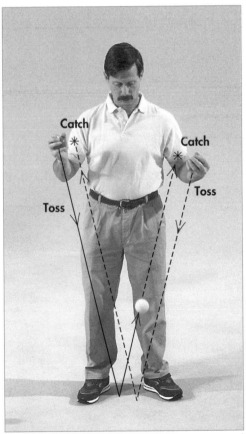

Figure 3.34   Catch toward the center and toss outside the ascending balls.

Toss down and immediately raise your knee; as soon as the ball passes under your knee, straighten your leg.

While juggling in the air, you can toss one ball extra high and let it bounce back up. Just hold the other two balls and wait. When the bouncing ball comes back up and begins to fall, imagine it is the first ball in a cascade pattern and start juggling again.

If you are juggling bouncy balls, you can retrieve a drop by stepping hard on the ball as it bounces away, pulling your foot in toward you at the same time. The errant ball will bounce up and back, high enough to work it right back into your routine.

Unicycle Riding

Now that you're a pro at three-ball juggling, why not learn how to ride the unicycle so that you can combine the two for an impressive routine. You may be thinking, Easier said than done! But with a lot of practice, as well as patience, you can master the unicycle!

You can find an inexpensive unicycle on our Web site.

Before you begin, keep the following safety tips in mind:

- Always wear shoes to protect your feet and ankles.
- When you first start, wear a helmet and biking or skateboard safety pads.
- Keep your tires fully inflated to make riding easier and safer.
- Stay away from cars.

Learning to Ride

You will learn best with two patient spotters. Use your spotters' arms to help keep your balance at first. You hold onto them palms down; they never hold onto you. Do not put your weight on your spotters; keep it on your legs. Use your spotters less and less each time you practice.

If you don't have spotters, use a fence behind you to mount and hold onto a wall or a railing to keep your balance.

Use spotters to help keep your balance at first.

Start to mount by holding the seat between your thighs. Step down onto the lower pedal when it is slightly toward the rear. The wheel turns back toward you and the seat post comes up until it is directly under you and straight up and down (a).

As you step down, bring your other foot up to the other pedal and push it forward while transferring less than half your weight to the seat (b).

Once on the seat, you must pedal forward constantly. Sit up straight and stay directly over the wheel, but let your center of balance lean ever so slightly forward. Pedal just enough to keep your center of balance over the seat.

a   *b*

Mounting solo (a and b).

Tricks and Stopping

To turn, lean in the direction you are turning. To go backward, lean ever so slightly backward. Use spotters at first. To dismount, step off forward, then reach behind and grab the seat so that it doesn't hit the ground.

Impress the audience by combining unicycle riding with three-ball juggling.

Now that you can juggle three balls, it's time to start carrying your juggling balls with you everywhere you go. Every time you have a moment—at the bus stop, in the movie line, at the airport, or wherever you are whether alone or in a crowd—take them out and practice. You will notice exciting things start happening when you become a juggler.

Practice looking through your pattern so you can look around at the audience. Involve them by tossing a ball out and asking them to toss it back. Use the ball they toss as number one in your pattern. Now that you are developing your skill, it's time to start working on showmanship. Learn to juggle to music or tell jokes while juggling or simply chat with the impromptu audience. If you are having fun, they will have fun too.

chapter

4

Four- and Five-
Ball Juggling

As soon as you perform with three balls, someone in your audience will
ask, "But can you do four?" And as soon as you are proficient with
four, someone will ask, "Can you do five?" So it is important to keep pushing
yourself forward and at least learn to flash the next higher number. A flash
means simply tossing each of the balls up once in the appropriate pattern
and catching them, as opposed to a juggle, which means going for two
rounds and catching successfully.

32 • *Basic Four-Ball Patterns*

At first, four balls are just two in each hand, with each hand doing its own
work. There are three basic four-ball patterns in which the balls do not
cross. At first, toss with both hands simultaneously so that you have two
balls paralleling each other in the air. Then you can learn to alternate your
hands. Remember to keep everything flat in front of you as if you were
juggling on a pane of glass. Don't shovel in toward yourself.

Outside Circles—Learn the outside circles first. They are the easiest. Toss two balls, one from each hand, at the same time in oval patterns from the center toward the outside. When they peak, throw the next two. Catch and scoop in toward the center and toss again. Every time two hit their peaks, toss another two right behind them on the same pathways. All your catches are on the outside, and all your tosses are from the center, arcing out. See figure 4.1. Next, alternate your hands: right, left, right, left.

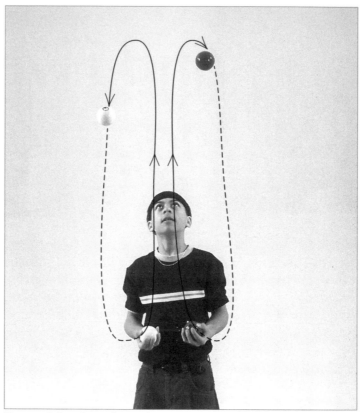

Figure 4.1 Outside circles.

*B*ecause collisions and crossed beanbags are common with outside circles, use two balls of one color in your right hand and two of another color in your left hand. Don't let the colors change hands.

Inside Circles—Next, try tossing inside circles that go along oval pathways from the outside toward the center, as shown in figure 4.2. Catch toward the center, scoop out, and toss back up the outside, arcing into the center again. Practice with one hand, then the other, then both hands. Practice simultaneous and alternating throws.

Figure 4.2 Inside circles.

Columns—Next, try columns or elevator shafts in which each ball has its own pathway. At first you can send two together up the outside and then two together up the middle. However, it will probably be easier if you alternate your hands with this pattern, as shown in figure 4.3.

To perform "splits," lean slightly to the left and toss two balls up the left side, then lean slightly to the right and toss two up the right side, as in figure 4.4. Lean back to the left and catch and toss again; lean to the right and catch and toss again. Widen your splits for maximum audience effect. The secret is to keep the tosses in a plane in front of you and to toss to the same height every time so that the balls come down together.

When juggling four in any pattern, first try to toss with both hands simultaneously, then try to toss alternately, right, left, right, left, but remember that each hand does its own work. Because the peak of the ball from each hand is the cue for that hand to throw again, your tempo is faster than it is when you toss two at one time.

Figure 4.3 Columns with alternating right-left throws.

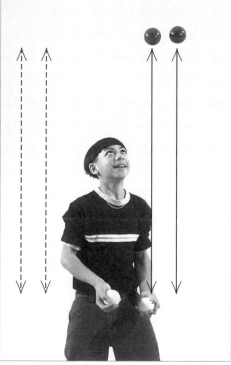

Figure 4.4 Splits: Ben has just tossed two balls to the left. Next, he will lean to the right and toss the two he is holding.

33 • Crossing Patterns With Four Balls

Holding two balls in each hand, throw one from each hand simultaneously so that they cross. The dominant hand should throw a bit higher. See figure 4.5. When these two balls peak and begin to fall, toss the other two balls.

Start with simultaneous tosses as in the previous pattern, but gradually bring your left hand tosses lower and lower until they are about the height of your typical cascade. The right hand throws keep going higher, and the tempo changes. Now every time you catch a ball, you toss it immediately. This is the half shower with four balls.

Figure 4.5 When crossing four balls, the dominant hand should throw a bit higher. Every time two cross, throw the next two.

34 • Mixed Patterns With Four Balls

You can mix all of your patterns with four balls, giving some interesting variations. For instance, you can toss outside circles with one hand and inside circles with the other. Walk sideways in the direction that these circles are going and they look like two big wheels moving one way. When you reverse them, the wheels seem to go the other way.

Toss two balls straight up simultaneously. Then toss two across in big arcs, again simultaneously. Alternate tossing two straight up and two across. Remember, when the balls cross, send one higher than the other so that they don't collide.

35 • *Multiplex*

Multiplex is a method of juggling many objects by throwing two, three, or more at the same time. With multiplex you can juggle four or five balls very soon after learning three. First we will focus on one relatively straightforward pattern for juggling five balls, and then we'll go over the different multiplex tosses so that you can invent your own moves.

Start with two balls lined up in your right hand (figure 4.6a). Point your fingers toward the midline. Toss the two balls at the same time. The one on the fingertips goes higher and farther, and the two balls split in the air (figure 4.6b). Catch one in each hand. Catch with the right hand first, then the left.

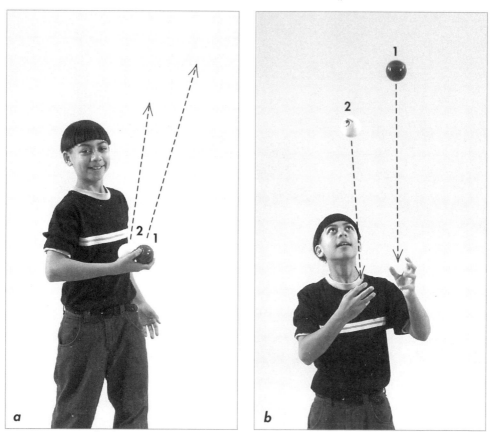

Figure 4.6 Multiplex: *(a)* start with two balls; *(b)* toss and split them in the air. Catch right, then left.

Now put one ball in your left hand and two in your right. Throw the two balls and split them. When they get to the peak, toss the solo ball from your left hand up and across, through the split. In figure 4.7, balls #1 and #2 are tossed at the same time and split. Ball #3 goes through the split. Ball #1 ends up in the left hand, and balls #2 and #3 in the right.

Now do this same series from the opposite side. Just use "right" for "left" and vice versa in the directions given.

Figure 4.7 Multiplex: Throw two balls and split them, then toss the third ball through the split.

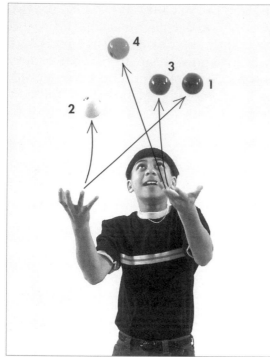

Figure 4.8 Multiplex with four balls.

Now hold two balls in each hand. It helps if they are numbered, variously colored, or otherwise different so that you can easily distinguish among them. Toss and split the two from the right hand (balls #1 and #2 in figure 4.8). When they peak, toss and split the two from the left hand. Learn to toss the left hand first and the right hand first. No matter which hand starts first, both the fingertip balls cross to the other hand. The balls from the heels of the hands come back to the hands where they started.

Now you can keep going with five balls. Start by tossing the solo ball from your fingertips in the hand that has three. After that first throw, every throw is a split of two, and you always throw that split between the two balls that are in the air. There are always two balls in the air and two on the way up. Alternate your hands, just as you do when juggling the cascade.

Don't try to understand this. Just do it!

Variations of multiplex—Stacking is throwing two balls at once from one hand so that they line up vertically in the air. You can stack two balls vertically and catch them in your opposite hand. You can juggle three in one hand by tossing two stacked, then one, catching the two stacked and tossing them again, then catching and tossing the one. You can toss three balls out of one hand and have them split so two come straight back down and one crosses to the other hand, or two cross and one comes straight down. Now, just use your imagination and put together your own astounding multiplex routine.

36 • *Five Balls the Easy Way*

First, get a partner who can juggle three balls. Start with five beanbags that you will share. Face your partner and throw to him slowly, as Dorothy has done in figure 4.9. Count out loud as you throw. The beanbags all cross in a high, slow cascade. Your partner simply catches the beanbags one by one.

Now your partner tosses back to you in the same manner and you just catch. Go slowly at first. Keep your pattern, maintain your peaks, and build up your tempo as you toss back and forth for each other. Don't back up; just share a juggling space. Don't use the peaks as a cue to toss, just toss as quickly as you can, maintaining accuracy.

Figure 4.9 Dorothy has just tossed five balls to Ben who catches them one at a time in the order thrown.

Once you can toss all five beanbags before your partner catches the first one, you are ready to go solo. Now stand on a hardwood floor in a quiet room and toss all five as fast as you can (figure 4.10a). Listen to the plops and note where they fall. A good tempo means equal time between plops. A good pattern means the beanbags are close to one another on the floor, with three on one side and two on the other, as shown in figure 4.10b.

Figure 4.10   *(a)* Toss five balls and *(b)* note where they fall.

Now that you have built up your speed and have good peaks, you can start catching.

1. Get five beanbags of different colors so you can tell them apart in the air.
2. Toss all five quickly in order and catch #1, but let #2, #3, #4, and #5 crash.
3. Start again, but this time catch #1 and #2 and let the others crash.

4. Next time catch #1, #2, and #3, but let #4 and #5 crash.

5. Next catch the first four in order, but let #5 crash.

6. Next catch them all in order, from #1 to #5.

7. Now toss them all again, and as soon as you catch #1, toss it again. It should end up back where it started, on the fingertips of your dominant hand.

8. Now just go for one more throw each time and one more catch. Once you can do 10 throws and catches, you have been twice around and are ready to keep going with five balls. Keep breathing normally and keep your shoulders relaxed. Maintain your tempo and maintain your peaks. Resist the temptation to reach up to catch.

With the five-ball cascade you do not get your tempo from the peaks as you did with three and four balls. When you're juggling five balls, your tempo comes from the descending balls. You must clear each hand before the descending ball gets to it so that you have an empty hand to catch and toss again. Your job is to start the five balls into motion at equal speeds and equidistant from one another along an elongated infinity sign pathway, as shown in figure 4.11. Then you must keep these five balls moving at the same speed and keep them the same distance from one another on the infinity sign path that you have created.

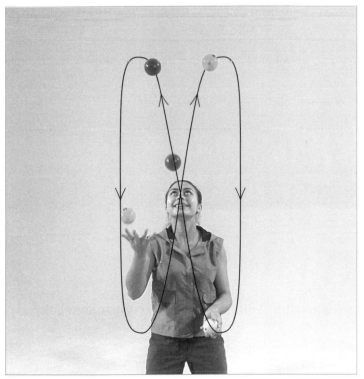

Figure 4.11   Five-ball cascade.

When you juggle two, three, or four balls, you look at the peaks since they provide your cue for the next toss. With five balls simply gaze at the entire pattern, seeing as much as you can, with the center of your visual field on the point at which the balls cross. Since maintaining the peaks is the key to maintaining the pattern, you do need to notice the peaks, but you also need to notice when balls are coming down from the peaks. With five balls your cue to throw is when each incoming ball is about a third of the way from the peak to your hand.

37 Half Shower With Five Balls

We will assume that you are right-handed for this description. Start with three balls in your right hand and two in your left hand. Start by tossing quickly, right, left, right, left, right. All right-hand throws go in a high arc over your head to the left hand. All left-hand throws go in a smaller "cascade" arc to the right hand. See figure 4.12. Once you get started, every time you touch a ball, immediately toss it along the proper pathway. At all times you should have three balls in your overhead arc and no more than two in the smaller cascade arc. Once you can maintain the half shower from your right hand, try it in the opposite direction, tossing over

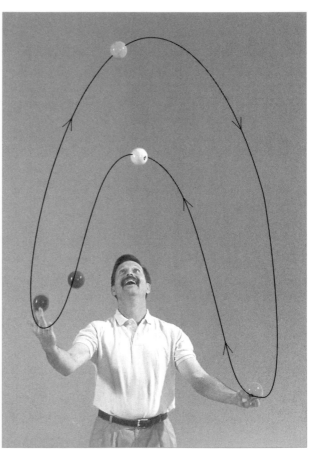

Figure 4.12   Dave juggles the five-ball half shower with big outside tosses from the right and smaller inside tosses from the left.

in a big arc from the left and under in a smaller cascade pattern from the right.

38 • *Reverse Cascade With Five Balls*

Once you can do a half shower from each side, the reverse cascade or "full reverse" is relatively easy to learn. The problem is keeping track of the balls as they fall down the center. Use five different colors to learn this move. If you can keep track of the order in which you throw the five colors, you can keep your catches in order. Every ball goes up the outside and down the center, as shown in figure 4.13. As with the five-ball cascade, the objective is to maintain the pattern simply by keeping the balls an equal distance apart on your infinity sign pathway. The cue for the next throw is not the peak, but the descending ball. You must clear every hand before the next ball arrives. Do notice your peaks, however, and maintain them. The tendency is for the pattern to get bigger and bigger as the peaks wander outward. Higher is better than wider, so if you need more time, raise your peaks.

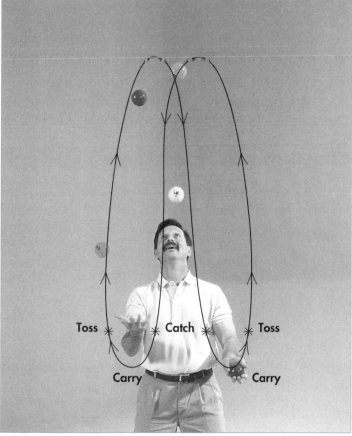

Figure 4.13   In the reverse cascade with five balls, every ball goes up the outside and down the center.

39 ● *Tennis With Five Balls*

Once you have a half shower from both sides, tennis is possible. Start with a five-ball cascade. Toss one of the five balls over the top to the other hand in a big reverse cascade throw. When you catch it, immediately return this ball over the top and back along the same pathway. Keep it low, just over the top of your pattern. Since that ball goes farther, you need to hurry the reverse cascade throws with the "tennis ball" and maintain your tempo with the other four.

Jugglers' tennis with five balls is hard for the audience to see unless you have one ball that is extremely different from the rest. When you perform with five balls, a single marked ball will help the audience to see and appreciate all the patterns.

40 ● *Shower With Five Balls*

Start with four balls in your dominant hand and nothing in your nondominant hand. Toss the four balls quickly along a high arc and catch them all in your nondominant hand. You need to work on your speed until you can throw so quickly that the first catch comes after the last release. Say, "throw, throw, throw, throw, catch, catch, catch, catch." Don't worry if you don't actually have room in your hand to catch the fourth ball—just make sure you touch it. If you want to catch it, however, it lands on the middle of the triangle formed by the other three balls.

Now try the same move, but hold a fifth ball in your subordinate hand. Just before you catch the first ball, pass the fifth across to the dominant hand and catch the four. Say "throw, throw, throw, throw, pass, catch, catch, catch, catch." Your pass across should be a very short throw; don't just hand the ball across. Catch with your palm slightly turned toward the throwing hand so that you are ready to toss up immediately. Don't claw the incoming ball with your palm down.

Start again with four in one hand and one in the other, as shown in figure 4.14a. Toss your four balls quickly and start passing the balls across from your nondominant to your dominant hand (figure 4.14b). Now, every time a ball comes to your nondominant hand, pass it across to the dominant one, and every time a ball comes to your dominant hand, throw. Say, "throw, throw, throw, throw, pass and throw, pass and throw, pass and throw." You actually need to move faster than you can speak, but the verbal cues will help you remember what to do.

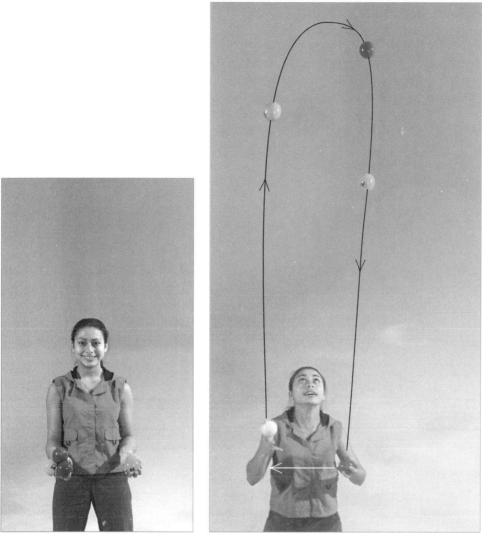

Figure 4.14 Five-ball shower: *(a)* start with four balls in the right hand and one in the left; *(b)* toss each ball quickly along a high, narrow arc. Pass from left to right with a short toss.

41 • *Six Balls*

If you can juggle five balls, you can certainly learn to juggle with six with only a few hours of work, so you may as well go for it. As with four balls, there are two rhythms to use when juggling six: simultaneous throws and alternating throws. Outside circles work best with six, eight, and ten objects. First, work on tossing fast with three in one hand in a long oval going from the center toward the outside (figure 4.15). Do this in each hand, then in both hands. Try both simultaneous throws and alternating throws and decide which works best for you. Figure 4.16 shows alternating tosses with six balls. The balls travel up the center and out to the sides. Try to go twice around before stopping so that you can say that you actually juggle six, rather than simply flashing them. Keep your peaks directly over your shoulders and don't let the pattern widen too much. Maintain your rhythm by tossing to exactly the same height every time, and try to keep both sides symmetrical.

When you first see someone juggling five or six balls, it looks impossible and you say, "I could never do that," but if you just dedicate one hour a day to juggling, and if you go step by step, you will be juggling five. So turn off the TV and practice. It's great exercise and you'll always have something to do!

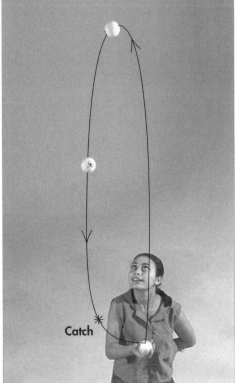

Figure 4.15 Six ball warmup: Three in an outside circle.

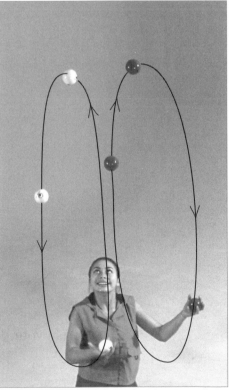

Figure 4.16 Six balls with alternating tosses, up the center and out to the sides.

chapter 5

Ring Juggling

Ring juggling is just like ball juggling, except you can toss higher and your hand catches in a V with the thumbs pointed inward. Giving the ring a spin as you toss it stabilizes the ring in the air. Unlike ball juggling, in which you keep your hands low, you can reach up to throw and to catch rings. Rings are generally 13 inches in outside diameter. To start, get rings that are different colors so that you can tell them apart in the air and the audience can appreciate your patterns.

42 • *Cascade With Three Rings*

Start with one ring and toss it back and forth from hand to hand with two nice high peaks. Once you have defined the pathway, toss two in a nice high X. To hold three rings, put two in your dominant hand. The one on your fingertips, held loosely between your thumb and first finger (figure 5.1), is the one you throw first. For now, start tossing in a high cascade, hitting those two peaks every time.

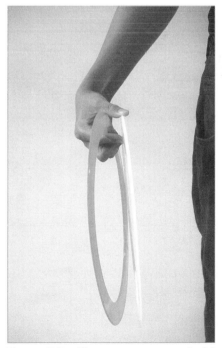

Figure 5.1 The proper way to hold two rings in one hand.

43 ● Spin a Ring on a Ring

To spin a ring on a ring, pinch the ring you want to spin between the fingers and thumb of your dominant hand. Don't throw high; instead, snap your wrist and get lots of torque on the ring. First try it without juggling. Just hold a ring flat in your nondominant hand and toss the spinning ring onto it. After you can spin the ring, learn to toss it with that same hard spin when you are in the middle of your juggling pattern, to the same height as the rest of the rings in the pattern. Catch the other two rings one in each hand and hold the one in your nondominant hand flat, making a solid platform on which to spin. See figure 5.2. Once the ring has spun and slowed down, toss it back into the pattern from its upright position on the ring in your nondominant hand.

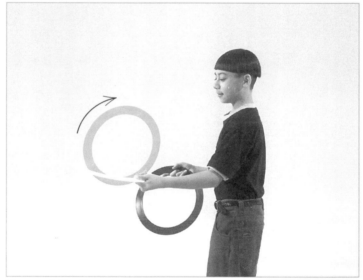

Figure 5.2 To spin a ring on a ring, don't throw high; just snap your wrist.

44 ● Flats

If you are facing the audience, you can turn the rings so that they are flat on a plane in front of you. You can juggle the cascade, with your palms in toward you (figure 5.3), or the high reverse cascade, with your fingers pointing up and your palms facing away. First practice with one ring, then two, and then three. Concentrate on the transition from a regular cascade to these audience-pleasing moves.

Figure 5.3 If you're in front of an audience, you can turn the rings so they are flat in front of you.

Rings look best from the side, so either juggle sideways to the audience or learn to throw rings so that the flat sides are toward the audience even when you are facing forward.

45 • Pancake Flips

You can flip rings like pancakes. Start by learning to toss one ring from hand to hand with your palm up and the ring turning a single flip up and toward you. Keep your four fingers straight out and flat and your thumb on top of the ring to stabilize it. Then learn to cross two rings in this pattern, one from each hand. To toss three, you will need to start juggling in the cascade and then turn your palms up and go right into the pancake flip (figure 5.4). Try a series of tosses from one hand first, then the other, and finally flipping every ring from each hand. This move lends itself to a great finale with one, two, or three pancake flips going right over your head and ending up around your neck.

Figure 5.4 In pancake flips, the rings flip just as coins do in a coin toss.

46 • Back Spin

You can also toss a ring away with a back spin and have it return to you on the floor. As it rolls toward you, integrate it back into your pattern by simply bending over and picking it up into a juggle. You can also try bouncing it back up into the pattern with your toe or find another imaginative way to keep juggling. If you do put this move into your performance repertoire, remember to test your stage first to make certain that you know what the rings will do since every floor is different.

47 • Tomahawk Chops

You can toss a ring or do a series of throws with rings from just behind your ear in a tomahawk chop. First learn to toss one ring from your nondominant hand precisely up to the tomahawk position, just behind your ear on the opposite side. Catch that incoming ring with minimal hand movement, just cocking your hand back after the ring arrives. A gentle nudge is all you need to toss the ring from your shoulder down and across your chest to your other hand. For the toss, your wrist should be cocked all the way back, and the ring pushed slightly forward and a bit up.

With two rings, start with one in the tomahawk posi-

Figure 5.5   Dorothy has just tossed the dark ring with a tomahawk chop and is about to catch the light-colored ring.

tion and the other in the normal throwing position. Practice starting with either ring. Make certain you keep your upper hand in the tomahawk position at all times. To juggle three, start in the cascade and move your catching hand up to the tomahawk position as you throw from your other hand to that position. Your instinct is to bring your hand back down from the tomahawk position, but you must leave it up there and continue throwing from there. Now every right-hand throw is a tomahawk chop, and every left-hand throw must come right up to the point behind the right ear. In figure 5.5, Dorothy has just tossed the dark ring and is about to catch the light-colored ring.

48 • Pull-Downs

When you are finished with your ring juggling routine, you can pull all the rings down over your neck for a dramatic finish. This move can be learned easily with three rings and can be used very effectively in your repertoire at every level up to six and seven rings. Simply catch high and bring the rings down over your head as you catch them, slowly for three and faster for higher numbers. Barely brush your ear with your knuckles as you bring each ring down so that you don't catch your ear on the opposite side, and pull slightly forward so that you don't crunch your nose. Practice the move first with just one ring in each hand so that you learn to avoid hitting your nose, ears, or glasses.

49 • Color-Changing Rings

To add a "magic touch" to your routine, you can make your rings appear to change color. To perform this skill, paint one side of your rings, glue two rings together, or put sticky-backed Mylar or shelf paper on one side of each ring. There are two ways to change colors. You can switch your hand around while it is waiting for an incoming ring so that you catch the ring with your palm up and your thumb out. Twist the ring inward so that it falls into the normal throwing position and toss again. A more difficult and more subtle method is to reach

Figure 5.6 Color change: Dave is catching the dark ring so it will flip over on its own.

through the ring as it falls and let the momentum of the descending ring pull it around (figure 5.6). Either way you can really surprise the audience with this seemingly "magic" trick. If you do the color change with the hand that is on the side away from the audience, most people will never see the move.

50 ● *Four Rings (and Six)*

To juggle four rings, start with two in one hand and learn outside circles. Then learn inside circles and columns, not only because you will juggle four in these patterns, but also in order to learn to adjust bad throws. As with four balls, each hand works with two rings, and you throw either simultaneously or alternating. The alternating pattern looks better from the audience's point of view. Of course, you stand sideways to your audience so that they can see the flat side of the rings.

When juggling an even number of rings, use outside circles. For six rings practice three in one hand with outside circles, then three in the other hand. (Hold three rings in your hand as shown in figure 5.7.) When you toss with staggered throws as in figure 5.8, the rings are easier to control because you can keep a narrower pattern and you are only doing one thing at a time. This pattern looks much better to the audience than simultaneous throws since the air seems to be full of an unbroken stream of rings.

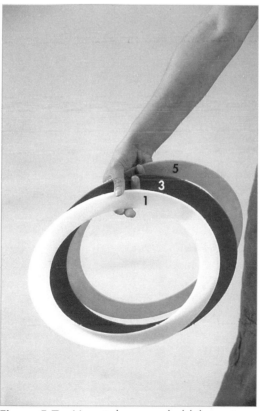

Figure 5.7   Here is how you hold three rings in one hand when you want to juggle five or six.

Figure 5.8 Juggling six with alternating throws.

51 • Five Rings (and Seven)

Learn to juggle five balls first. The pattern for five rings is the same, but you toss higher. Hold three rings in your dominant hand as shown in figure 5.7. Keep your peaks separate and as precise as possible. Learn to release the three rings from your dominant hand in succession first, then try all five. High and slow is easier than low and fast because the rings take up more space than balls, so collisions are a factor.

When practicing with five or more rings, consider wearing tight-fitting nylon or spandex gloves or taping the last knuckles of your little finger and ring finger where rings rub on the release. If your hands get chafed when practicing with five or more rings, put A&D ointment on the web between your thumb and index finger after practice to help them heal.

Rings are colorful and have much more audience appeal than balls. They are the prop of choice in the quest to juggle large numbers of objects. You can pass rings with a partner, but clubs are the best prop for passing, so it's time to move on to them.

chapter

6

Club Juggling

All juggling clubs commercially available today are made of plastic, either solid or cellular foam. They are either inexpensive one-piece clubs, which are mass produced, generally in Asia, or they have many parts and are laboriously pieced together on a workbench in Europe or North America. The handcrafted clubs generally have a wooden dowel down the middle and an air space between the dowel and the plastic covering, giving them soft handles. We recommend that you begin with an inexpensive set, preferably of three different colors so that you can learn the basics and sort out the paths of various clubs within patterns by watching the sequence of the colors.

Jugglebug sells an inexpensive set of three plastic one-piece clubs with soft, molded knobs and butts that are durable and great for learning the basics. You can get them at magic stores, kite shops and toy stores, or from our Web site. These clubs cost about one-fifth as much as a set of three handmade clubs purchased from a prop maker.

You should consider buying soft-handled clubs when you begin passing, when you juggle with four or more clubs, or when you begin trying advanced club tricks that require high throws and multiple spins. By this time you will know whether you want to get long-handled clubs (about 20.5 inches) or short-handled clubs (about 18.5 to 19 inches) and whether you want a wide-bodied American club weighing about 9 ounces or a slimmer European model weighing as little as 7 ounces.

52 • Club Cascade

Start with one club in your right hand. Hold it at a 45-degree angle away from your body. Hold the club like a tennis racket, by the handle, not the knob. Place your thumb about where the handle begins to widen. Scoop that club under as if you were tossing under a microphone in front of your face. The butt of the club makes a U in the air. Release as your hand reaches the center of your body.

The club should make a single flip and end up pointing to the left at a 45-degree angle. Now scoop back under the microphone and flip the club once back to the original hand. While you should start by tossing high and slow, eventually this entire pattern can be moved down below eye level. Explore the space in front of you with one club following this infinity sign path. This should become a relatively effortless flowing movement with the momentum of the body of the club pulling it down in a scoop and back up again. Use your wrist, elbow, shoulder, and upper arm to redirect the club. Relax your shoulders and resist the temptation to reach up to catch.

To exchange two clubs, hold one club in each hand at a 45-degree angle. Toss the club from your right hand with a scoop under that invisible microphone. As it peaks and turns, throw the second club with a symmetrical underhand scoop in the opposite direction and under the pathway of the first club. Catch the first club by the handle, not the knob, with your left hand and catch the second club with your right. Pause and repeat.

Now you're ready for the complete cascade with three clubs. Hold one club in each hand, but place an additional club in your right hand, with your index finger extended along the neck of that club, as shown in figure 6.1a. Now, just as you did juggling three balls, start with the hand that has two, alternate your hands, and go for two throws. See figure 6.1b. Learn to catch the second club on top of the one in your hand without dropping. Learn to catch in a way that requires no readjustment before throwing again.

Now go for three throws and learn this final catch in your nondominant hand. At this point you can learn to start from either side. Just put two clubs in your nondominant hand to start. Try to juggle along for a set number of tosses and catch cleanly.

Start juggling high, about two feet above each shoulder, but bring it down so that you can eventually juggle below your eyes. This is especially important when you start passing clubs and need to look at your partner's eyes and notice the entire pattern. As time goes on, widen your pattern, use more wrist and forearm to juggle the clubs and less shoulder and upper arm. Experiment with using your thumb to push down on the handle, giving the club a faster spin and reducing your efforts even further. Move your hand out to the end of the handle and experiment with using your thumb as a fulcrum at the base of the knob to give the club a more effortless spin.

Figure 6.1 Cascade with three clubs: *(a)* starting position; *(b)* every time one club spins, throw another, and keep alternating your hands.

To get the feeling of continuously juggling with three clubs, you may want to juggle two balls and one club for a while. Start the club in the solo hand and the balls in the other. Toss the ball on your fingertips first. When you are ready to move one, don't bother with two clubs and one ball. It is easier just to go for three clubs.

If your clubs collide, widen your pattern or slow down your tossing. If you can't catch your clubs accurately, go back to two and practice the exchange until it feels natural, then try three again. If you run forward while juggling, or if you hit yourself in the chest, reestablish the plane in front of you by going back to two clubs and making wider scoops. Then go back to three, but keep everything on that flat plane in front of you.

Immediately after learning to keep three clubs going, experiment with one and a half, double, two and a half, and triple spins. You should learn the feeling of each of these spins so that you can toss them randomly at any time or toss them continuously with either hand. This experimentation will help you later on when you may toss an erratic club and need to recover and keep going.

53 • *Under the Leg*

Start by tossing one club back and forth with a single flip under the right and left leg, from both the right and left hand. Now try the move while juggling. Start by throwing every third right-hand club under the right leg (figure 6.2). It may help to toss the previous one a bit higher than usual to gain some time. Try every second club, then continuous throws with the right hand under the right leg, keeping that leg in the air. Learn the same move on the other side, left hand under left leg. Now learn right throw under left leg, and left throw under right leg. Finally, you may be able to toss a club under either leg with every throw, jogging in place as clubs fly up from under your knees.

Figure 6.2 Tossing under the leg.

54 • *Over the Head (Reverse Cascade)*

Throw with a high, wide arc. Toss either single or double flips. First start the cascade. Using your dominant hand, toss one club in a high arc over your head, pause a bit while it takes this extra long journey, and toss the next club with your nondominant hand, back into the cascade pattern. Try a series of over-the-head tosses from your dominant hand, and then try a series from your nondominant hand. Once you can toss over from either hand, try both right and left hands. See figure 6.3.

Figure 6.3 To do the reverse cascade, throw each club in a high, wide arc. As you gain skill, reduce the height of the tosses.

When juggling clubs, learn early to relax your shoulders and use your wrists to throw rather than hunching up your shoulders and tossing with your whole arm.

55 ● Floaters

In this move the club crosses your body along the usual path, but it doesn't flip end over end; it just seems to float over to the other hand (figure 6.4). To toss a floater, first learn it with one club. Your dominant hand will probably find this trick much easier than your nondominant hand. To keep the club from flipping, hold it high on the neck with your thumb on the body of the club and give it a spin for stability by rolling it off your fingertips. If you toss an occasional floater, you can toss dramatically with the body high and the knob down so that the club is almost vertical. However, if you toss a series of floaters from both hands in the cascade pattern, you'll need to really work on catching high on the clubs and keeping them all horizontal to avoid collisions.

Figure 6.4 The floater club doesn't turn end over end; instead it rotates on its linear axis, which helps keep it from flipping.

56 ● Columns

Learn to toss double spins straight up and down with one club. Learn this in each hand and then practice with two clubs at the same time, one in each hand. The trick is to keep the spins even with the two clubs so that they go to the same height, turn together, and come down at exactly the same time. Next, learn two clubs in one hand with double spins. Keep each in its own pathway, with the clubs going up and down parallel with each other. Now learn the pattern in your other hand, with the same parallel pathways.

You now have the parts needed to put the whole pattern together.

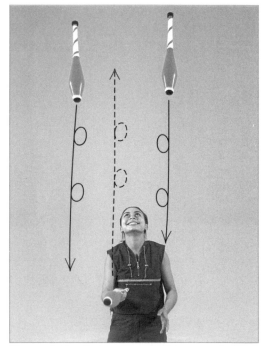

Figure 6.5 Columns with clubs must be precise, with both hands tossing to the same height at the same time with the same spin.

Start with the cascade, and when you are ready to start columns, toss one club straight up with a double spin. As it peaks, toss the other two up with double spins in their own parallel pathways (figure 6.5). The usual pattern is the same as with three balls, one up the middle and two up the sides, but experiment with tossing the solo club in different ways: up one side, over the top, up the other side. Eventually work on splits in which you toss one club up one side and two up the other in an ever-widening gap. This is a very difficult trick but a great crowd-pleaser.

57 • *Four Clubs*

The moves you learned for columns are the key ingredients for four clubs, so why not work on that trick now. The main difference is that for columns you toss straight up, but for four clubs you generally make outside circles. First, work on outside circles with two in one hand and then with two in the other hand. Try to toss simultaneously at first (figure 6.6a); then alternate right, left, right, left (figure 6.6b). Alternating throws are probably easier to catch since you don't have to do two things at once, but you may feel you need to move faster. We'll come back to four clubs later, but it is worth trying four now since you will use the same high double spins for many different tricks.

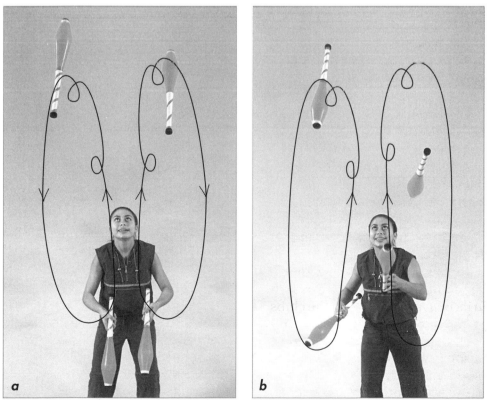

a   b

Figure 6.6   Juggling four clubs with *(a)* simultaneous throws and *(b)* alternating throws.

58 ◦ Pirouette

Try this move first with scarves, then with balls, and finally with clubs. The juggling is easy; turning yourself around and reentering the routine is the hard part. It is recommended that you "spot" as dancers do. Turn your body first, and then have your head follow, turning rapidly around to the front again and looking up at the last moment to catch. Start with just one club, toss it up with a double spin, notice it at the peak, then pirouette and catch it in your other hand. Once you can do this consistently, hold two, toss one up with a double spin, and just as you finish your turn, toss the other one across with a single spin and catch the first club you threw in your empty hand. Now try holding three, toss one club straight up with a double spin, pirouette (figure 6.7), and start juggling. Finally, try the pirouette out of the cascade. Toss one club high with a double spin, spot the club for an instant, and pirouette rapidly, holding the

Figure 6.7 Toss the club with a double spin, then pirouette.

other two. When you get around, toss one club up and across your chest under the descending club, catch that solo club, and renew the cascade.

59 ◦ Three-Club Start

Hold three clubs with two on top, one below, and the lower club knob held by your fingertips up under the handles of the upper two clubs, as shown in figure 6.8a. Throw all three. The center club does a high triple spin and the two side clubs do double spins, not as high (figure 6.8b). Catch the two clubs simultaneously. When the solo club comes down, start juggling.

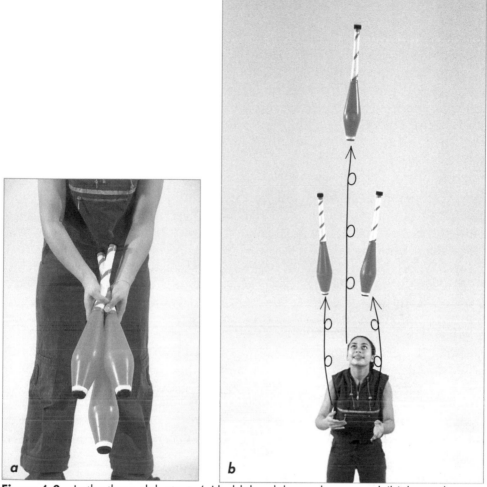

Figure 6.8   In the three-club start, (a) hold the clubs as shown, and (b) throw them so that the center club turns three times and goes higher than the other two, which turn twice.

60 • *Under the Arms*

You already learned this skill with balls. As before, you should begin by learning the basic move. Start with two clubs in your dominant hand. Cross your arms, reach under your opposite wrist with your dominant hand, and toss club #1 straight up. Then uncross your arms and toss across your chest from the nondominant hand, which clears that hand to catch the descending club. Now you can just go into the cascade with three clubs. Learn to go under your wrist occasionally by tossing every second or third club under the wrist and uncrossing your arms to catch and continue. Learn the same move on the other side with the other hand.

Now just remember a marked club. Start with two clubs in your dominant hand, the marked club on your fingertips. Reach under your opposite wrist and start by tossing the marked club straight up, then uncross your arms and toss across your chest from the nondominant hand. This clears that hand to catch the marked club. Toss the next club across from the dominant hand and reach under the wrist of the dominant hand with the nondominant hand and toss the marked club straight up, moving your nondominant hand back quickly to where it came from to catch the incoming club. Now every time the marked club lands, reach under the opposite wrist and toss it straight up. The other two clubs are simply juggled in a cascade pattern.

61 • *Chops*

Start with one club in each hand. Carry the club in your right hand up and back down in a big arc, toward your left hand. As your right hand chops down toward this new position, toss the club from your left hand under the wrist of the descending hand, then toss the club from your right hand in a short throw toward the left. The clubs have crossed because you carried the club across instead of throwing it. Separate your hands and catch both clubs.

Now try the move once while continuously juggling in the cascade pattern. Chop with the right hand in a big arc, toss the club from the left hand, crossing under the wrist of the right hand and into the cascade pattern, then throw right, left, right, left, and keep juggling. Now try the move continuously with your right hand, as shown in figure 6.9a. After you catch club #1 with the right hand, chop across while you throw club #2 with the left hand under the right wrist. Then toss #1 in a short throw to the left and move your right hand back to catch club #2 (the one that was thrown by your left hand under the right wrist), catch the chopped club in the left hand, and repeat.

Figure 6.9 *(a)* Right chop,

(continued)

Figure 6.9   *(continued)* and *(b)* left chop.

Now learn this same series from the other side, as shown in figure 6.9b. Once you can chop on each side, learn to do chops on both sides in succession. Every club that crosses your chest is chopped, and every throw is straight up, under the opposite wrist.

To deepen and widen your chops dramatically, toss all your throws as high and as wide as possible while still maintaining the pattern. Slide your grip on the club handles down to just above the knob to lengthen the path of the chop and swing the club quickly and violently down to the lowest and widest possible point. Bend forward slightly at the waist and bend your knees rhythmically, turning your body slightly in the direction of each descending chop. Remember to keep the bodies of the clubs moving in arcs that are flat to the audience to enhance the look of this move.

62 • Back Crosses

1. Start with one club and toss it back and forth over the far shoulder with a single spin. Reach way up to toss, and slide your hand down to the knob to assist you in getting a high throw with plenty of spin.

2. Start with one club in each hand. Toss from your right hand over your left shoulder. When you see the incoming club, toss from the left hand. Catch both clubs, pause, and repeat. Practice the same move starting with the other hand.

3. While juggling three clubs, toss an occasional right-hand throw over your shoulder. Eventually you should be able to toss every other right-hand throw. Once you can toss every other from the right, learn it from the left, as shown in figure 6.10. This over-the-shoulder throw can be a great trick in itself.

4. Once you can reliably toss every other throw over the shoulder with either hand, shift back to the right hand and work your way up until you can toss every right-hand throw in succession over your left shoulder. Then learn this move with the left-hand throws going over the right shoulder.

Figure 6.10 Back crosses: Left-handed toss over the right shoulder.

5. While juggling three clubs, toss two in a row, one over each shoulder. Once you can do this reliably, go for a third toss, and then a fourth.

6. Count every throw. Keep a record of your success, and every practice session try to exceed your previous best. When you can toss 100 straight back crosses using both hands, you have learned the skill solidly and will not lose it.

7. Once you can toss back crosses with single spins, try double and triple spins. With single spins you need to turn your head quickly from side to side. The higher you throw, the slower the pattern, and the less you need to turn your head.

Use soft or lightweight clubs when you learn back crosses. Practice turning your head from side to side and practice the arm motions without any clubs. Remember that you only get to see the club for a microsecond as it comes over your shoulder, not when you catch it. In that microsecond you have to spot the club and make any adjustments to catch it. Practice is the key to this move.

Give yourself two to three hours per day for a week to learn this move. It is hard, but worth the effort in terms of personal satisfaction and audience appreciation. Top-level professional jugglers can even do back crosses with five clubs.

63 • Balancing a Club

While juggling three clubs, reach up quickly and balance a club by the knob on your chin or forehead, as in figure 6.11. Balance for a while with your arms outstretched to get applause. You can toss one of your other clubs across and drop the one that is balanced into the empty hand and resume. To learn this trick, first learn to balance a club on your chin or forehead, then learn to balance one while holding another, toss, and drop. You can then learn to start juggling from the balance. Finally, learn to quickly put a club up for the balance while juggling.

Figure 6.11 Try balancing the club on your forehead.

64 • Kick-Ups

Start with one club. Rest it on your foot with the handle pointing inward and the knob across your ankle and shin. As you kick up and back, flex your foot, as shown in figure 6.12. The sharp edge of the knob of the club should catch your shin, and the club should do a single flip to your hand. Once you can do one club from one foot, learn the other foot. Then hold a club in your dominant hand and kick another one up to the same hand from that same foot. Learn to toss the one in your dominant hand at the same time that the one from your foot peaks and finishes its turn. Do this move until it is smooth.

Figure 6.12 Pick up with a kick-up.

Next, put one club in each hand and rest one on your right foot. Give a kick with the right foot, toss right, then toss left, and you are juggling. This trick really helps when you are passing clubs and want to get a club back into the pattern without bending over or stopping. You can eventually learn to find a dropped club by quickly glancing down, roll it onto your right foot with your left, and kick up into your own pattern to fill the space of a dropped club without breaking the rhythm of passing. Finally, learn to drop a club to your foot while you are juggling, cradle it on your foot, and kick it back up into the pattern again.

65 • Fancy Finishes

Toss one club high with a double spin. Transfer the club out of the catching hand by passing it across. You can either hold it in your opposite hand parallel with the other club, or you can clamp it under your arm with the knob out. Then catch the double-spinning club in the empty hand.

Toss one club high from the right hand with a double spin. While it is in the air, transfer the club from your right hand to your left, as in figure 6.13a. Grasp the two clubs tightly. Make a V between these two clubs in your left hand. Thrust forward hard to catch the third club between these two, trapping the handle and the knob (figure 6.13b).

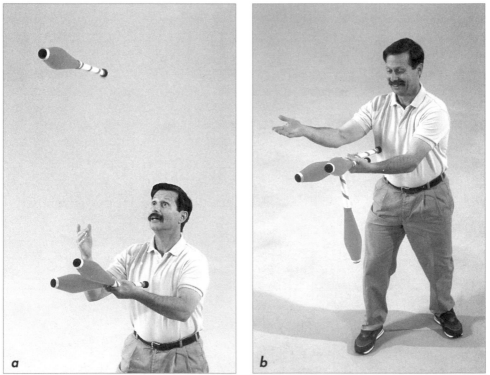

a   b

Figure 6.13   For a fancy finish, *(a)* toss one club with a double spin, transfer the club that's in your right hand to your left, and *(b)* trap the club in the other two.

66 • *Five Clubs*

Before you try five clubs, practice five balls or rings for a while, tossing higher and more slowly than usual to establish the five-club rhythm. Now, toss one club back and forth from hand to hand with high double spins.

Next, hold two clubs, one in each hand, and toss them one at a time in an X with high double spins. Practice starting with either hand first. Now hold two clubs in one hand and one in the other. Toss them in order with high double spins: right, left, right. Catch all three and then toss back left, right, left. Next, hold two clubs in each hand. Toss right, left, right, left with these same high-crossing double spins. Catch two in each hand. Then toss left, right, left, right.

Now hold three clubs in your dominant hand, as shown in figure 6.14. Learn to toss the first club from your fingertips with an extra push from your pointer finger. Practice throwing these three one at a time with double spins, catching two in the other hand and letting the third fall.

Now is the time to practice your special finish. Start with three clubs in your dominant hand. Toss all three, the first two with double spins and the third with a triple spin. As soon as you have caught your first two clubs in your other hand, tuck them quickly under your throwing arm and reach out and catch that final club in your empty nondominant hand (figure 6.15).

Figure 6.14 Holding three in one hand.

Figure 6.15 Finish by tucking two clubs under your throwing arm, then catch the third in your empty hand.

Hold your five clubs with three in one hand and two in the other. Toss all five: right, left, right, left, right (figure 6.16a). Catch the first four in order: left, right, left, right, and let the fifth club fall. Now do six throws, catch four clubs and let the sixth throw fall to the ground. Go forward one more throw each time, letting the last toss hit the ground. Once you can go for a run of about eight or nine throws, it is time to begin catching the last club with the special finish we practiced previously. Decide when you are going to stop. Toss your last throw with a triple spin. Catch two in your left hand and tuck them under your right arm. Catch the last club dramatically with your left hand. If you do this right, you will already be kneeling and taking a bow (figure 6.16b).

Here is an exercise that some jugglers use to improve the start, clearly define the peaks, and encourage continuation: Start with three clubs in one hand. Toss them in order and, without stopping, throw each one back as soon as it is caught. Keep alternating hands: three throws in a row from the right, three throws in a row from the left. Practice ending with the finish described earlier.

a   b

Figure 6.16   (a) Juggling five clubs and (b) taking a bow.

Torch Juggling

Once you can juggle clubs well, you can juggle other linear objects such as specially manufactured juggling knives, machetes, or torches. As jugglers, we rely on our hands and eyes to make a living, so we would never do anything to jeopardize either. Prop makers manufacture knives that are made to look sharp although they are dull. Torches are designed so that when they are dropped the wick is never in contact with the floor. Both knives and torches are specially balanced to make catching the handles easy.

Safety Tips

- Buy professionally manufactured torches designed for juggling.
- Kids should have adult supervision.
- Have a fire extinguisher and water source handy.
- Do not juggle in flammable clothing. Avoid synthetics, which burn quickly.
- Make certain there are no flammable curtains or furniture under which a dropped torch might roll.
- Tie up long hair. Avoid hair spray that is highly flammable.
- Locate the wind and make sure it is at your back.
- Ensure that you are a good distance from your audience, especially children. They will not know what to do if a torch flies or rolls their way, or if a burning wick flies off the torch.

Torch juggling is a surefire way to impress an audience. (No, Dorothy's hair is not on fire.)

Torch Juggling Technique

1. Pour a small amount of white gas or camping fuel into a plastic cup.
2. Dip your torches; don't soak them.
3. Shake the residue off violently.
4. Pour the leftover fuel from the cup back into the original container and screw on the cap.
5. Remove the fuel to a safe distance.
6. Light one torch and use it to light the others.
7. When not juggling, hold the torches with their wicks up.
8. If you catch the wrong end, let go quickly.
9. When finished, shake your torches violently until they go out.
10. Do not try to refuel torches until they are cool to the touch.
11. Torches are filthy, so wrap them in plastic when not in use.
12. Breathing the vapor from burning torch fuel may be hazardous to your health, so avoid prolonged exposure.

Juggling linear objects like clubs and torches adds a level of difficulty and a level of skill to your routine. It puts you in a pretty exclusive group and shows that you have paid your dues. Now it's time to learn interactive juggling so you can share in the infinite varieties of passing patterns.

Partner Juggling

Once you can juggle three balls or three clubs, it is time to find or to develop a partner. In terms of audience appeal, a partner routine is usually far more impressive than a solo routine. Also, working together is more than twice as much fun! It takes patience, but develops it as well. You

can learn all of the interactive routines with scarves or balls first and then work on the same moves with clubs. Remember to laugh occasionally, and never blame yourself or your partner for drops. Nobody is perfect, and you learn to juggle drop by drop.

67 • Side by Side

The easiest way to juggle three balls with a partner is to stand side by side. Put your arms over each other's shoulders. Now both of your outside hands can act like the two hands of one juggler (figure 7.1). Just remember that the

Figure 7.1 Stand side by side so your arms act as the two hands of a single juggler.

person with two balls starts, then alternate between you and your partner. The biggest problem with working side by side is that your partner's tosses may go out in front. Just remind him that he should keep the throw in, and do the same yourself. Establish two peaks on a flat plane in front of you and hit those peaks every time. Then you can play with the pattern. Toss under the ball that is in the air and you are doing the cascade; toss over and you are doing the reverse cascade. While your partner juggles seriously, you can reach up behind his back and give him "bunny ears," a proven kindergarten crowd-pleaser.

68 • Front to Front

Now try the same trick facing your partner about five feet apart with one hand behind your back. One person holds a ball in the left hand. The other person holds two balls in the right hand. The person with two balls starts by tossing one to the partner. Now all you do is toss back and forth, with a pretty high arc. Toss with an arc across to the opposite hand, not diagonally. Every time one ball gets to the peak, your partner tosses the next one under it with an equally high arc (figure 7.2). After you can pass with your right and your partner's left, try it with your left and your partner's right. Resist the temptation to back up.

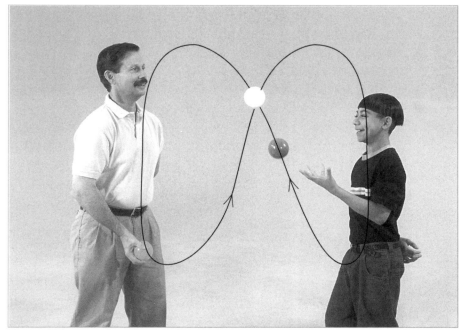

Figure 7.2 Juggling face to face.

In a performance you can make one of the audience members look very good by tossing balls back and forth with this pattern. Start with two and give the audience member one. You can even use basketballs since you use two hands to hold, to catch, and to throw the balls. You toss one, she tosses one, you toss one, she tosses one. In a very short time you can teach the move and demonstrate the pattern.

69 ● *Take-Away From the Front*

Face your partner and get close so that you share a juggling space. Your partner starts juggling with three balls, preferably of three different colors so that you can tell them apart and agree on what each of you will do. For instance, you can say, "When the red ball comes toward my right hand, I'll reach up and catch it," and your partner will know which ball you are talking about. Your job is to keep three balls going in a cascade pattern, but to switch jugglers.

Start by juggling with a nice high pattern. Make a mental note of the ball that you want to catch first. When your partner throws it from his right to his left, reach up high with your right hand and take that ball off the top of his pattern right at the moment it peaks.

Now you are committed to take all three. Immediately after taking the first ball with your right hand, reach up with your left hand and take the second ball, the one coming from your partner's left hand and headed for your right (figure 7.3). Take it at the peak also. At this point you have one

Figure 7.3 Ben (right) has been juggling, and now Dave reaches in and takes the balls one by one as they reach their peaks.

ball in each hand. Your partner's responsibility is to toss the third one up the middle, across to your right hand, along the pathway it would normally have followed. Your responsibility is to keep your hands out where they won't get in the way of this third ball. When that third ball peaks, toss the ball from your right hand along the cascade pathway and catch the third ball. All three balls now belong to you, and you are juggling them in the same order and to the same peaks as was your partner. There is no break in the pattern; only the hands doing the juggling have changed.

Once you can take three balls from the front, you can take them with style. Grab aggressively with your palms up, or claw with the palms down, or even snatch them off the top with your palms facing outward. Once you feel comfortable sharing this juggling pattern, you can simply remove one ball and drop or toss it back into the pattern. Your partner keeps juggling the two remaining balls, but keeps the space for the third ball. You find the space and replace the ball with style.

70 • Take-Away From the Side (the Run-Around)

Once you and your partner can both come in from the side and take over a juggling pattern, you can run around each other sharing three objects. The objects keep moving, but the juggler changes.

To start, learn to step in boldly and take over the pattern. Your partner juggles three. You come in from his left, reaching up with your left hand to take the ball intended for his left. Reach up high and take it at the peak. As soon as you have the ball in your left hand, reach rudely across with the right hand and catch the next ball, the one intended for his right. Now you have a ball in each hand. Freeze and let him throw the third ball between your outstretched hands, on its normal path, toward the left, as in figure 7.4. As soon as this third ball peaks, toss from your left hand and continue the juggle. Your partner moves out and you move in. Now he comes around behind you and moves in from your left, taking over just as you did. Once you can complete a run-around, you can go faster and faster until your last throw is the first one you catch.

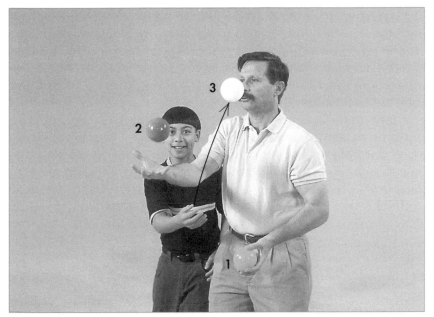

Figure 7.4   Ben (left) was juggling and Dave moved in from his left and took #1. Then as Dave reached across with his right hand to get #2, Ben tossed #3 into the pattern.

Once you have control of this trick, you can slow down the pace and add other elements, for instance: take your partner's hat, take a towel draped over his shoulder and a carrot from his mouth, and then take the balls. Now you can create a complete story with character development and a dramatic ending, juggling side by side with your arms over each other's shoulders, sharing the hat, the towel, and even the carrot. Just use your free inside hands to move these items back and forth between you while your outside hands continue to juggle the three balls.

71 • *Running Three Balls*

This is a lead-up to passing six objects and is a great way to learn passing routines without having to worry about drops.

Start juggling three balls facing your partner, about six feet apart. After your pattern is stabilized, toss one of your right-hand throws with a high arc across to your partner's left (figure 7.5a). At the next instant you have a ball in each hand and can pause if you need to, and so can your partner.

Next, you toss ball #3 across your chest from your left to right hand, at your own speed. When that ball peaks and begins to fall, toss the next right-hand throw (#2) across to your partner's left hand following the same high arc (figure 7.5b). When ball #2 hits the peak, your partner tosses ball #1 from his left to his right hand. At that same moment you are tossing from your left to your right. Your partner catches your second throw and now has one in each hand. Now your third right-hand throw (ball #3) goes across from your right toward his left along that same arc, and as it peaks, he takes over the pattern and juggles all three balls until he is stabilized and ready to toss them back to you (figure 7.5c).

In running three continuously, the balls make a rectangle from your left, to your right, to his left, to his right, and back to your left. Remember to alternate your hands and to throw all right-hand throws to your partner and all left-hand throws across your chest.

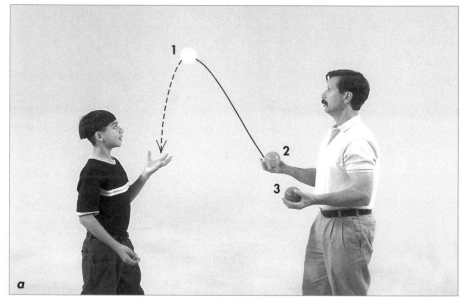

Figure 7.5 In running three, every right-hand throw goes across to your partner's left. All your left-hand throws go across your chest from left to right.

(continued)

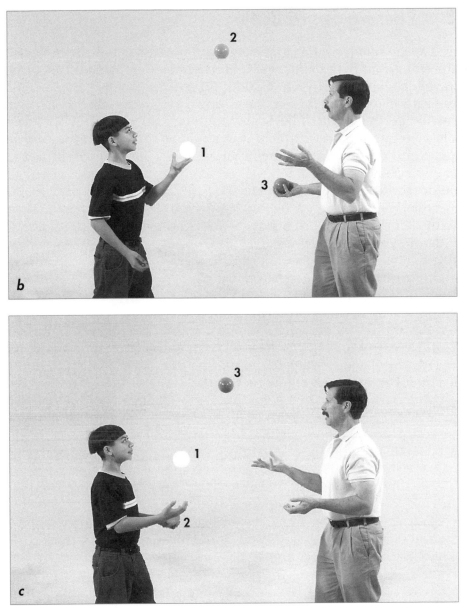

Figure 7.5 *(continued)*

72 • *Passing Six Balls*

The most common six-object passing pattern is called "3-3-10." Every third ball leaving your right hand is passed across to your partner three times. Then every second right-hand ball is passed across three times. Finally, every right-hand ball is passed 10 times. Everywhere you go in the world, you will find that jugglers know this routine. Your pattern is a rectangle when seen from above, with all of your left-hand throws going across your chest and some of your right-hand throws going across to your partner's left.

Before trying to pass six balls with a partner, make certain your patterns and timing are the same. Juggle facing each other and keep the same rhythm. Bring your pattern down and look through it. You should be able to juggle low enough that you can look at each other's eyes. Eventually you can get "in-sync" and just notice the passes and catches with your peripheral vision.

To learn as easily as possible, you and your partner should each use a similar set of three balls with three different colors. If you each juggle three balls that are red, yellow, and blue, and if you set your hands up the same way and start at the same time and with the balls in the same positions, it is easy to see if you are juggling together. Both the red balls go up at the same time, then both the yellow, then both the blue. The balls are held with two in the right and one in the left to start. Each of you holds a ball of the same color in your left hand. To begin passing, both you and your partner raise your hands shoulder high (figure 7.6a), lower them at the same time, and begin juggling the cascade at the same time and to the same height, starting with a right-hand toss. Figure 7.6b shows each person tossing at the same time from their right to their partner's left, following a rectangular pathway when seen from above. (See figure 7.7.)

In the following count, "hup" means bring your hands down, numbers represent right-hand self-tosses, and "and" represents left-hand self-tosses. "Throw" means to toss with a gentle arc from your right across to your partner's left. This ball takes the place of the one your partner would have thrown for himself from his own right hand if he had just kept juggling.

The full count for 3-3-10 goes: "Hup, one and two and throw, and one and two and throw, and one and two and throw, and one and throw, and one and throw, and one and throw, and throw, and throw, and throw, and throw, and throw, and throw, and throw, and throw, and throw, and stop."

Step 1 is to practice the start and the first three throws across to your partner. This start is called "slow start," and the rhythm is called "every thirds" or "six count." Face each other and raise your hands. One of you chants the following as you practice: "Hup, one and two and throw, and one and two and throw, and one and two and throw." The ball that started out in each person's left hand goes across from each person's right hand to the partner's left hand.

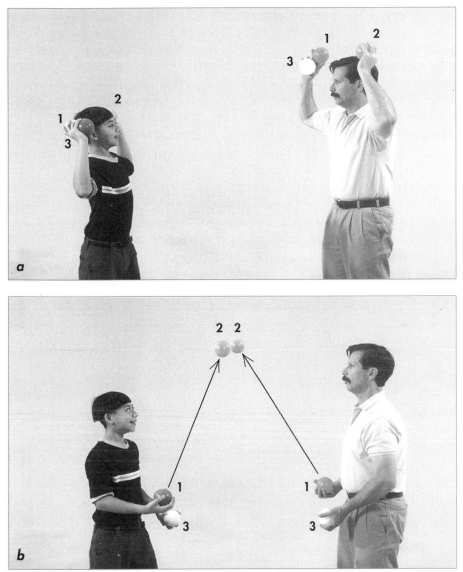

Figure 7.6 Passing six balls: *(a)* starting position; *(b)* tossing simultaneously from your right to your partner's left.

Step 2 is to practice "every others," throwing every second ball across, also called a "four count." Practice this second step right after the first, without a break. If you set your hands up identically with the same color balls in the same positions, you and your partner will be throwing the same colors across at the same time. Work on putting these first two parts of the entire pattern together until you can do them almost every time.

Step 3 is to add the last 10 throws, which are called "solids" or "every-ones," with every right-hand throw going to your partner's left hand and every left-hand throw going to your own right hand.

Work through the whole routine together and go as far as you can each time. It may take a few hours, but eventually you will be able to complete 3-3-10 over and over again. Remember to repeat the full count to give you the verbal cues you need to pass. Eventually, the count becomes your mantra, and you can internalize it and say it silently and subconsciously.

You may find that your left-hand throws are mimicking your right, and you are tossing toward your partner with your left hand instead of across your chest. To overcome this habit, practice alone facing a corner where two walls come together. Recite the count and toss right-hand throws high and straight so that the ball will bounce twice, once against each wall, and return to your left hand following about the same trajectory as a partner's ball would follow. Your left hand only tosses across your chest to the right hand.

73 • Passing Seven Balls (or More)

If you can pass six, you can pass seven. When you are passing six (or eight), you and your partner keep the same rhythm and toss and catch at the same time. With seven (or nine) your individual juggling rhythm is the same and so is your partner's, but you can't look at or rely on each other for the rhythm, as you will be one beat off. In other words, whenever you are tossing with your right hand, your partner is tossing with his left. The only problem is getting started with odd numbers since the person with the most objects must start first. Once you are passing seven, there is no noticeable difference to either of you except that you are tossing a bit higher than with six. The balls still follow a rectangu-

Figure 7.7   The balls follow a rectangular pathway, as seen from above.

lar pathway when seen from above, with all of your left-hand throws going across your chest and all of your right-hand throws going across to your partner's left (figure 7.7). However, from the audience's point of view it looks much harder because the pattern is asymmetrical and there appear to be a great many objects in the air.

First you need to learn a "live" start. That means your first throw is a pass to your partner, not a self-throw. Learn the live start with six balls so you can start immediately passing with no "warm-up" throws to yourself. Each of you holds three, with two balls in your right hand. Toss the fingertip ball to your partner in a nice high arc along the passing pathway you have developed. Then toss your left-hand throw to yourself. Just keep tossing "solids" or "every one," with all of your right-hand throws going to your partner and all of your left-hand throws going to yourself.

Now, on to seven. One of you starts with four balls, two in each hand, and the other starts with three, as shown in figure 7.8a. You don't need to raise your hands to start since you don't start together. The person with four tosses the fingertip ball in the right hand across, throwing just a bit higher than usual. The other juggler starts one beat later, when the incoming ball is halfway across, with a similar toss across from the right to the partner's left. As soon as each of you tosses your first throw, start juggling, left to yourself, right across and passing in the "solids" pattern, keeping your own rhythm, which is one beat off from your partner's (figure 7.8b). In other words, you are tossing with the left hand whenever your partner is tossing with the right hand. All throws, your self-throw and your toss across, can be a bit higher in order to slow the pattern down.

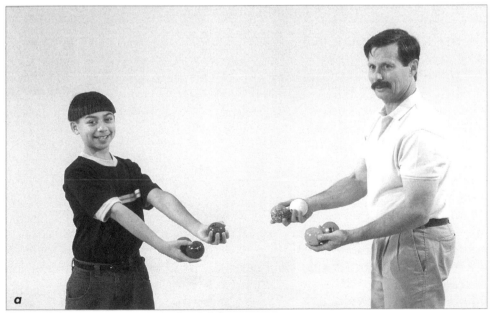

Figure 7.8   Passing seven balls: *(a)* the start;

(continued)

Figure 7.8   *(continued)*   and *(b)* alternating throws with your partner.

The big temptation with seven balls is to toss with both hands simultaneously. Count cadence quietly to yourself, "left, right, left, right" to stay on the beat. Because you are not in rhythm, avoid looking at each other for visual cues about when to pass. Just make certain that you keep your own rhythm. Both of you need to learn to start with four balls, so that when you drop, either of you can initiate the pattern again.

With odd numbers, one of you will always start with one object more than the other person. The person with more objects always goes first. If you toss higher, you don't have to go that much faster; just keep the consistency of your tosses so that your margin of error is reduced. If you can juggle five balls, you can pass eight or nine with an equally skilled partner.

74 • Passing Six Clubs

We will assume that you and your partner have learned to pass six balls using the 3-3-10 routine described earlier. Even if you have not passed balls, in a short time you can pass six clubs by following these directions precisely, starting with one club, going to two, then to four, back to three, and on to five and six.

One Club—Throw one club with a scooping underhand toss across your body from your left to your right hand. This self-toss is called a "vamp." The club turns once, and you catch it approximately in the middle of the handle. Keep your palms up. As you catch, drop your right hand down and back so that the club hangs parallel to your right leg with the body of the club down and the knob up. Bring your arm up toward the front and release the club at between waist and chest height. Your thumb acts as a fulcrum. The club rotates one and a half turns and ends up in your partner's upraised left hand, knob down. This pass is called a "single" since the club apparently turns once in the air. Your partner throws from left to right and passes back to you. Run one club through this pattern until you can do so smoothly, then move on to two.

Two Clubs—Each of you holds a club in your left hand. Simultaneously toss from left to right, then pass across to your partner's left, as described with one club. Repeat over and over until you get the feeling for passing across to your partner with your right hand and then catching the incoming club with your left hand.

Four Clubs—Each of you holds two clubs, one in each hand. Simultaneously, each of you tosses your left-hand club to yourself, and when it turns, you each pass your right-hand club across to your partner (figure 7.9). Catch the club you tossed from your left hand in your right hand, and then catch the one passed by your partner. The cadence is "throw left, throw right, catch right, catch left." Then pause and repeat. Practice this move until you can do it reliably, but don't get stuck here.

Figure 7.9 Passing four clubs: Ben and Dorothy have both just passed their right hand clubs across to their partner, then they each caught the club tossed from their own left hand in the right. Now they are preparing to catch the passed club with their left hands.

Three Clubs—This is "running three balls" described previously as skill 71. You start with all three clubs; your partner has none. Once you are juggling and are stabilized, pass a club to your partner from your right hand to his left hand. Then toss to your own right hand from your left hand and pass the next right-hand throw across to your partner. Finally, pass him the third club. Now he has all three and you have none for a while until he decides to pass them back to you. Breathe normally and throw slowly. You can pause as long as you like after you have passed any club to your partner. Gradually increase the tempo and eliminate any pauses.

In figure 7.10, Dorothy has already passed club #1 to Ben. Then she passed #3 across her chest and #2 to Ben. Next, he will toss #1 across from his left hand to his right and catch #2 in his left hand. Then Dorothy can toss #3.

Figure 7.10   In running three, each club turns once with every throw.

Five Clubs—Start by juggling three clubs; your partner holds two. When your pattern is stable, pass a club from your right hand across to your partner's left hand (figure 7.11) on the pathway you have been practicing. Now it is your turn to wait. When the club you have passed across to your partner peaks, she starts juggling alone by tossing from left to right. Once your partner is stable, she passes a club back across to you from her right hand to your left hand. With this system you can work on passing across to your partner without having to worry about juggling immediately

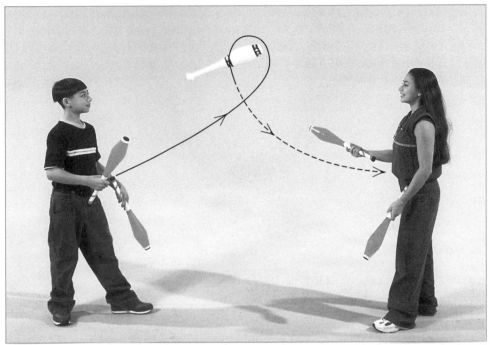

Figure 7.11   Passing five clubs: Ben has tossed the white club from his right hand across toward Dorothy's left. Next, she'll toss her left-hand club across her chest and catch the incoming white club.

afterward. Unlike running three balls, in which you have nothing to do half the time, with five clubs you each get to practice the same amount.

Six Clubs—Once both of you can pass one across to a partner out of the juggle and can start juggling when you receive the incoming club, it is time to move on to six. Start with three clubs each. Each of you should have a recognizable club (the marked club) in your left hand. Raise your hands and your clubs in a salute (figure 7.12a). Bring your hands down and start working your way through the instructions for passing six balls (skill 72).

Your stance in club passing is important. The right leg is slightly back, and your weight is evenly distributed on both feet (figure 7.12b). This way you will avoid hitting your right leg when you pull back to pass, and you will have maximum flexibility of movement when you need to chase an erratic toss. Throw with your full arm, including your shoulder, elbow, and wrist, but also use your thumb to push down on the handle of the club just above the knob.

Toss with a nice high arc so the club comes in gently. Try to make the same throw each time. Consistency is the key to success. Pass to your partner in a plane parallel to the side of your body with the knob and butt of the club turning in this plane, not tilted inward or outward. Minimize extraneous body movement. Smooth out your pattern. Gaze at your whole pattern by looking at your partner's face. Focus on feeling your throws and seeing your catches. Eventually, you can eliminate the arc and pass with more force and speed, but at the beginning you want to take it easy on each other, so pass with high, slow "lobs."

Figure 7.12 Passing six clubs: *(a)* the salute; *(b)* simultaneous throws from your right hand to your partner's left, after the count, "One and two and throw."

*T*here are many ways to hold your hand when catching a passed club. For most catches your elbow is down and the knob of the club is also down (figure 7.13a). When your partner throws with a bit too much spin, the knob may point up (figure 7.13b). Just catch and recover by tossing a one and a half to your other hand. If a chop is thrown to waist height, allow one-quarter additional turn and catch as shown (figure 7.13c). When your partner tosses a helicopter spin, catch it with your fingers pointed up or down depending on the direction of the spin (figure 7.13d).

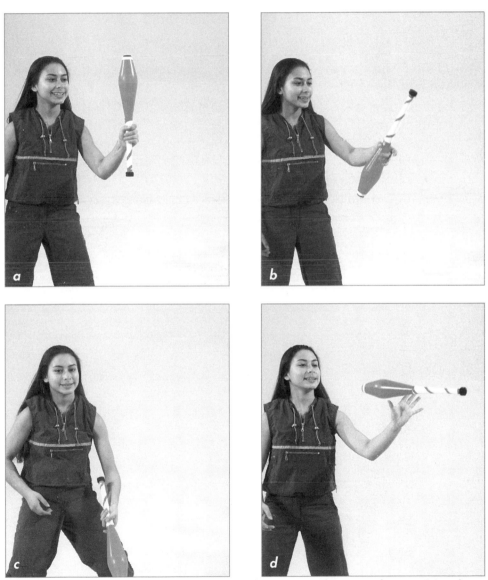

Figure 7.13   Catching (a) a normal pass, (b) a pass with too much spin, (c) a chop, and (d) a helicopter pass.

75 • Passing Tricks

You can learn fancy tosses and difficult catches while running three clubs. First, get rid of two clubs by passing them to your partner from your right hand, one by one; then throw the last toss with your fancy pass. You learn to throw these special passes without having to keep juggling, and your partner learns to catch the special throw and immediately begin juggling. Options include:

- Passing under either your right or left leg by raising your leg through the pattern (figure 7.14).
- Passing between your legs with feet planted.
- Raising your arm to toss an overhand chop and throwing gently, with just a nudge.
- Passing over your shoulder by holding the knob and letting the club rotate forward.
- Passing with a shoulder throw that comes from between your legs. Use the knob, bend way over, and reach deeply between your legs. The club skims past your shoulder. (See figure 7.15.)
- Throwing with a helicopter spin, either turning the club clockwise or counterclockwise. Cock your wrist way back, just like throwing a Frisbee.
- Passing a floater that does nothing at all. Hold the club with the body up and push it across to your partner by thrusting your arm straight out. As you release, give it a slight spin to keep the club stable in the air.

Figure 7.14 Passing under your leg.

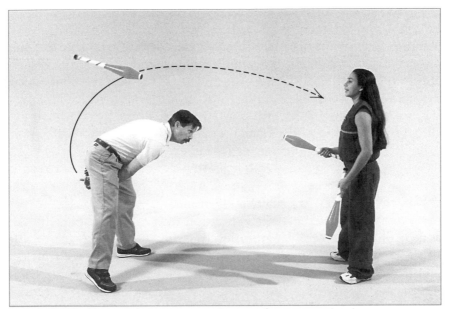

Figure 7.15 Passing between your legs and over your back.

○ Passing a double or a triple spin to your partner. Get the feeling for
each of these, as they will be useful later. The secret is not to turn the
club any harder; just turn it the same as for a single spin, but toss
higher. The club will turn the right number of times for the height you
throw. Once you learn to do a "live" start and pass six clubs in solids
with double spins, you are ready to pass seven clubs.

*W*hen you are running three clubs, think of all the things you can do to
*"ham it up" while your partner has the three clubs. You have time to clap, turn
a pirouette, or turn and blow a kiss to the audience. You can run over and hand
him the third club or just hold it extra long and turn it into an imaginary
spyglass, wooden leg, or canoe paddle.*

Once you have developed a repertoire of tricks while running three
clubs, it is time to do those same tricks while passing six. Be patient with
your partner. You can both invent and test different throws. For audience
appeal, work on doing the same passes at the same time. It is easier to
maintain your passing patterns in the "every other" or four-count rhythm
than with "every third" or "every one."

For extra credit, learn to go from every other to every one and back
again. Signal your intention to your partner by saying "hup" as you toss
with your left hand to yourself. Then do one more right-hand pass in the
old cadence and shift to the new one on the next right-hand toss.

76 ● *Passing Seven Clubs (or More)*

Before attempting to pass seven clubs, you and your partner should be able to pass six clubs with solids doing double spins, and you should go through the steps and learn to pass seven balls. If you are the person with four clubs, start by holding two in each hand. Toss the club on the fingertips of your right hand to your partner with a high double-spin throw. Your partner, holding two clubs in her right hand and one in her left, waits just a moment until that incoming pass hits the peak. As soon as she sees that the first club is at the top, she passes one club from her right hand across to you on a matching high arc, also using a double spin, followed immediately by a left-hand self-throw, which is a high single spin. See figure 7.16.

Now you are committed. Every left-hand toss is a bit higher than usual across the chest. Avoid the temptation to toss out and away from yourself with this throw by making a conscious effort to keep this toss in a plane right in front of you. Every right-hand toss is a high, slow double spin.

Club passing is the major recreational activity at juggling festivals and conventions. It is an endless pursuit with infinite variations limited only by human imagination. Now the challenge is to get together with other jugglers and explore the possibilities. Get videos of juggling shows and competitions and build on what you see. Good luck and happy passing!

Figure 7.16　Passing seven clubs: Throw with your right hand at the same time your partner throws with the left.

Devil Sticks and Diabolo

I f you've had fun with balls, rings, and clubs, and you are ready to take on a new challenge, devil sticks and the diabolo are great ways to add to your ever-expanding repertoire of manipulative skills. These ancient Chinese juggling props can be thrilling to watch and exciting to perform!

Devil Sticks

These ancient Chinese juggling toys, also known as juggle sticks, rhythm sticks, flower sticks, or angel sticks, became a counterculture icon in the 1970s and 1980s when they were frequently used to pass time at Grateful Dead and other rock concerts. You can buy a beginner set at any kite shop, toy or magic store, or on our Web site.

77 • Getting Started

Start by tossing your center stick back and forth, with your point of contact close to the top of the stick (figure 8.1). Toss and catch first with cupped hands, then with increasingly extended fingers so that you simply cradle the stick for a second and toss it gently back and forth with a slight upward nudge. The tip of the stick should trace an arc in front of your face.

Next, do this "windshield wiper" motion with one handstick and one of your empty hands. Finally, move on to two handsticks. Point your index fingers out along the handsticks. Your center stick probably has a knob or cap on the end that will allow your handsticks to catch it if it slips. Toss the center stick back and forth from handstick to handstick, as shown in figure 8.2. You should only touch the top half of the center stick.

Figure 8.1   Start by tossing the center stick back and forth with your hands.

Figure 8.2   Now use the handsticks to toss the center stick back and forth.

If the center stick is rolling or falling away from you, point the tips of your handsticks in a bit more. Keep your handsticks parallel and level with the ground. Remember, don't hit; just toss and catch.

78 · Flips

Experiment with half flips, full flips, one and a half flips, and double flips. Just toss a bit harder than usual so that the center stick goes higher and spins more (figure 8.3). Pull the other handstick out of the way until the center stick comes down. Absorb the momentum of the descending center stick on that other handstick and toss back. Learn the feel of a half, full, one and a half, and double flip from one side and then the other.

Figure 8.3 Learn half and full flips in both directions, then try one and a half and double flips.

Don't just stand in one place and hit your center stick back and forth. Move with the stick. Put on music with an exciting beat and move energetically from side to side as you hit the center stick back and forth. Make every move as athletic and outrageous as you can.

79 • *Airplane Propeller*

This is also a carrying move, not a hit. As you are tossing the center stick back and forth, pull out one of your handsticks and lower the point of contact of the other to about an inch or two below the center. See figure 8.4. Begin by making small tight circles around the center of the stick. Your driving handstick actually stays in contact with the center stick for about half of the rotation, pushing up and around with a small, gentle circle, as though you were stirring coffee. Eventually you will get "the touch" and can just keep spinning the center stick around and around.

Learn to circle your center stick to the right and to the left with each hand. Then you have plenty of ways you can spin, and you can combine them in interesting ways.

Figure 8.4   The center stick spins continuously around one hand, like an airplane propeller.

80 • *Helicopter Spin*

In this move you will eventually be pulling the center stick with one hand and pushing it with the other to keep it circling parallel to the floor. To get started, toss the center stick back and forth. When it is coming toward your right hand, reach out, make contact with it close to your right hand, and pull back toward yourself at the same time that you toss across. The center stick will begin to revolve in a horizontal plane. With your left handstick continue and increase the horizontal momentum. Make contact with the center stick close to the tip of the left handstick. Then push slightly away from yourself at the same time that you toss back to your right handstick.

The left handstick hits the bottom half of the cen-

Figure 8.5   The right handstick pulls the top half of the center stick and the left pushes the bottom half to cause the center stick to rotate parallel to the ground.

ter stick about one-quarter of the way between the center and the bottom end. Your right handstick hits the top half of the center stick about one-quarter of the way between the center and the top end. The right handstick pulls the top half of the center stick and the left pushes the bottom half of the center stick as you continue circling. See figure 8.5. Remember, the point of contact on the right handstick is very close to your hand; the point of contact on the left handstick is much farther away.

Once the center stick is rotating horizontally, you can pull your left hand out, leaving your right hand to tap up under the midpoint of the center stick, giving it a small amount of torque to continue the helicopter.

81 • *Under the Leg*

Toss the center stick back and forth, and as soon as it has left your right handstick, raise your right knee high and reach under it with the right handstick. Catch and toss the center stick with the left and hit back to the right, which is now under your right leg (figure 8.6). Catch and toss back from this position. Now you can either withdraw your right handstick and return it to the normal position or leave it under your knee for several successive hits. Practice on both sides. Eventually, you may be able to jog in place while hitting under your legs with alternating right and left hits.

Figure 8.6   Raise your knee high to toss the center stick back and forth under your leg.

82 • Behind the Back

Toss the center stick back and forth, and as soon as it has left your right handstick, reach behind your back with that handstick. Catch and toss the center stick with the left handstick and hit back to the right handstick, which is now behind your back coming out under your left arm (figure 8.7). Catch and toss back with the right handstick from this position. Now you can either withdraw your right handstick and return it to the normal position or leave it behind your back for several successive hits. Practice on both sides.

Eventually, you may be able to hit behind your back with your right handstick as described; then, as you return that handstick to its normal position on the right side, hit the center stick with your left handstick. Next, as your right handstick returns this toss, reach behind your back with your left handstick to catch the center stick. Continue if you can, alternating your arms behind your back.

Figure 8.7 Moving the center stick from the front to behind the back requires quickness and lots of practice!

83 ● *One-Stick Tricks*

Toss the center stick across with your right handstick (figure 8.8). Immediately pull that handstick back, reach across to where you would normally hit with your left handstick, and reinsert it in your pattern. Hit the center stick with a backhand stroke. Now every time you hit, you quickly shift your right handstick back and forth from side to side, tossing the center stick with alternating forehand and backhand strokes with the right hand. Your move across must be quick, but your hit must still be gentle. You can tap harder, toss higher, and get a full flip with your forehand stroke.

With one handstick you also can tap up alternately on the two ends of a horizontal and nonspinning center stick to keep it flat and parallel to the ground. From this move you can begin a succession of very slight taps in the exact middle of the center stick to keep it horizontal and not spinning.

Figure 8.8 Quickly shift your right handstick from side to side to toss the center stick back and forth.

84 ● *Kick-Ups*

There are two ways to kick up the center stick, the easy way and the hard way. The easy way is to drop the center stick onto your foot or roll it from the ground so that the center tape is over the center of your foot. Then kick straight up and catch it on the handsticks. See figure 8.9.

As you have discovered, jugglers like to try things the hard way. This time place one end of the center stick on your foot. Pull the edge of the cap on the end of the center stick back against your shin by flexing your foot. As you raise your foot, hook the stick with the top of your foot and kick upward and out to the side. The center stick should flip as it climbs, and you can catch it on the handsticks and keep it going.

Figure 8.9   Kick the center stick straight up, then catch it on your handsticks.

85 • *Twiddling*

Twiddle your thumbs. That is how your handsticks will move when you turn the center stick in a plane perpendicular to your body. Trap the center stick between the handsticks. Every time either of the handsticks comes toward your body, pull up on the lower half of the center stick toward your chin. Once you can turn the center stick in this upward and inward direction, try the opposite direction. Pull up on the outer end of the center stick, toward your forehead (figure 8.10). Either way, beware of the center stick.

Figure 8.10   Twiddling: Watch out for your chin!

F or style, right after hitting the center stick, you can toss a handstick, flipping it a half turn in the air. Catch the handstick with the same hand that threw it and get back in position to hit again. You can juggle the two handsticks and the center stick and then go back into devil sticking. Think of other ways to toss, balance, or pass your handsticks to make your routine more interesting.

86 • Partner Tricks

You and your partner each have one handstick. Toss one center stick back and forth, giving your partner the opportunity to catch it and look good at the same time (figure 8.11). Don't make your passes too hard, but do make them interesting. The objective is to keep the center stick going. You can also execute a run-around just as you did with three balls or three clubs, sharing one center stick and taking it over from each other as you walk and then run around and around each other (figure 8.12). The trick is to go faster and faster until you can each hit the center stick just once on each rotation. Toss high and slow for your partner and have her do the same for you.

Figure 8.11   Two partners sharing one devil stick set.

Figure 8.12   The run-around: Ben is about to come in and take over the center stick from Dorothy.

87 • *Training Wheels*

Unless you are using a professional juggling prop, your center stick has a cap on each end
that can help you to save tricks
by giving you "training wheels"
to use if the center stick begins
to slide away. See figure 8.13.
You can also use these training
wheels to spin the center stick.
The easiest way to spin is with
the center stick turning around
the handstick as shown. Once
the center stick is spinning, you
can toss it up into the air to turn
and to return to that same
handstick, or to go across to
the opposite handstick.

Diabolo

This ancient Chinese toy was
traditionally made of sections
of hollow bamboo, with slits

Figure 8.13   If the center stick starts to slide
away, you can use the caps on each end to
help regain control.

cut in the edges to create a whistling sound, and a wooden axle. Over the
last few decades of the 20th century the diabolo went through a metamor-
phosis, initially in Europe. It is now customarily made of two rubber or soft
plastic hemispheres fitted together using a metal axle. Beginning and
intermediate models can be found in kite, toy, or magic stores or on our
Web site. Once you learn the basics, European prop makers have many
models to choose from. The best diabolo string is 50 percent nylon and 50
percent cotton. Your string should be about as long as the distance from
the floor to your shoulder.

The moves we describe here are only a few of the hundreds of exciting
moves that ancient Chinese masters and modern diabolists have invented. They are intended to give you a basic repertoire that you can
expand by experimenting; by watching one of the many diabolo videos
available; or by attending diabolo workshops at local, regional, national,
or international juggling festivals. For audience appeal, work on moving
smoothly from trick to trick and keep moving your body to the left and
right as you perform these moves.

88 • *Spinning the Diabolo*

To Start the Spin—Since the diabolo only turns in one direction, your first task is to learn to start it in that one direction and keep it spinning. We'll assume throughout this chapter that you are right-handed, so just reverse these directions for left-handed spinning. Place the diabolo on the ground and over the string and pull the string slightly taught. Point your right handstick down to the center of the diabolo and hold the left handstick at about waist level. Take a step to the left, making an upward-slanting "ramp" with the left handstick and string (figure 8.14a). Now pull with your right hand and the diabolo will roll across the floor from right to left, seeming to go up the ramp.

To Maintain the Spin—Lower your left handstick slightly as the right handstick comes up. Now lower the right handstick way down and raise the left one slightly, just to keep tension on the string. Now the right handstick "whips" up while the left "drums" down (figure 8.14b). This movement is not symmetrical. The right

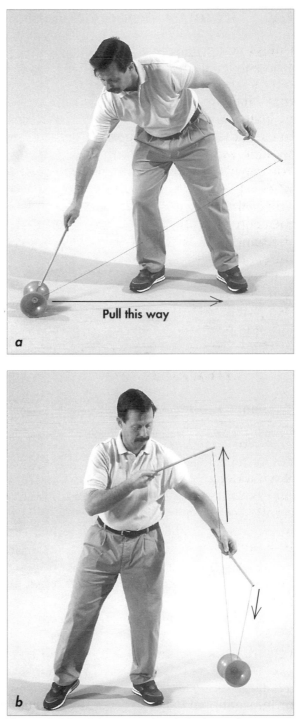

Figure 8.14 *(a)* to spin the diabolo, pull it across the floor from right to left; *(b)* to keep it spinning, give the right handstick a strong pull and lower the left one slightly to pick up the slack.

hand moves faster and higher than the left, with a whipping upward motion and a relaxed downstroke. The left hand drums downward and comes up slowly. As the diabolo spins, walk around so that you are always facing the flat or open side of the diabolo.

Your diabolo may tilt toward you or away from you. To prevent tilting, you need to understand that force is only transferred to the diabolo where the string is touching the axle. If the diabolo tilts toward you, tilt it away by pushing your right handstick forward, which makes the string gently touch the inside of the axle. If it tilts away from you, pull your right handstick back to nudge it back into balance with the string.

89 ◦ Tossing the Diabolo

a

Figure 8.15 *(a)* Raise and spread your arms, tightening the string.

(continued)

Figure 8.15   *(continued)*   *(b)* Catch the diabolo, then immediately bring your hands together to absorb the shock.

Get the diabolo spinning, then raise and spread your handsticks, tightening the string with a snap. The diabolo should fly high up into the air (figure 8.15a). Then look up, sight along your arm and the right handstick, and catch the descending diabolo near the right handstick on the tight string (figure 8.15b). At the instant that the diabolo hits the string, relax the string by bringing your right hand down and raise your left hand slightly to absorb the shock of the falling diabolo. For style points, you can execute a series of short tosses without a pause, or make a high toss and then jump over the string once or twice before catching.

90 • *Cat's Cradle*

To tie a cat's cradle as shown in figure 8.16a, first get your diabolo spinning as fast as possible. Switch your right handstick to your left hand and your left handstick to your right hand by passing the right stick under the left. Now, with your string crossed, point the right handstick slightly down and bring the tip of this new right handstick around, in front, and to the left of the left handstick. Return that right handstick string back toward the right side by pulling it over the midsection of the left handstick. Now insert the tip of your right handstick into the V-shaped gap created by the string. After your right handstick is partway in this opening, tilt both your handstick tips up in a vertical plane and the cat's cradle X should appear in front of you.

For the next stage, toss the diabolo from its current position under the X with a gentle upward thrust (figure 8.16b), sending it off the string and catching it, while spinning, on the top of the cat's cradle, in the center of the X.

To finish, tilt the tips of your handsticks down and inside, pointing toward a spot between your feet on the floor. The diabolo will drop down onto the string, unraveling the cat's cradle.

Figure 8.16   *(a)* First tie the cat's cradle, then *(b)* toss the diabolo onto the top string.

91 • *Whipping*

Whip your diabolo to make it go faster. Pull hard and fast across your body with your right handstick so that your right hand crosses over your left (figure 8.17). When the diabolo reaches the end of this pull, whip your right hand back to the starting position and repeat the move, but this time the right hand crosses under the left. The left hand simply keeps tension in the string. The right hand does all the work, and the diabolo spins faster and faster. This can be a crowd-pleasing trick in itself, or it can become a method for accelerating the diabolo.

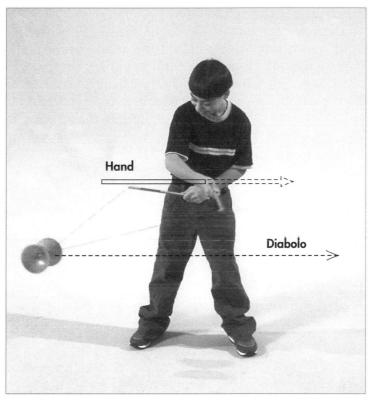

Figure 8.17 The diabolo flies from side to side as your right hand whips back and forth across your body.

Chinese Method—Loop your handstick around the axle of the diabolo. Keep your left handstick at about eye level. Lower your right hand, then whip it up and down rapidly, bringing the diabolo up and down. It accelerates rapidly with both the up and down strokes.

92 • *Over the Leg*

While the diabolo is spinning and on the center of the string, simply extend your right leg and push down on the string to the right of the spinning diabolo with your foot or calf. It may require a slight pull up with the left hand, but the diabolo will hop your foot or knee from left to right (figure 8.18) and you can catch it back on the string. Let the string go slack a bit and the diabolo will pass under your leg or foot on the way back to where it started. Learn to circle the diabolo around one leg over and over.

For a particularly impressive trick, step over the diabolo string and keep both feet planted while the diabolo circles your thighs, first on one side and then on the other (figure 8.19). The right handstick stays out in front and the left handstick stays to the back. Your left hand pulls up each time to make the diabolo jump from back to front. Shift your weight back and forth as your handsticks point alternatively to the left and to the right. Every time you lean your hips to the right, point both handsticks to the left as the diabolo circles your left leg from back to front, and every time you lean your hips to the left, point both handsticks to the right as the diabolo circles your right leg from back to front.

Figure 8.18 Making the diabolo jump over your foot or leg is a great crowd-pleaser.

Figure 8.19 Even more impressive is to circle the diabolo around your thigh.

93 ● *Climbing the String*

Accelerate the diabolo and, once it is moving fast, wrap the string once around the axle, raise your left hand, and pull hard, tightening the string (figure 8.20). The diabolo should climb the string.

Figure 8.20 To make the diabolo climb the string, loop your right hand around the diabolo and pull down.

94 ● *Stick Tricks*

You can also catch the diabolo on one handstick, let it spin for a while, and then toss it over or drop it to the other handstick and then onto the string. You can also catch the diabolo on crossed handsticks, as shown in figure 8.21. Use your handstick to adjust the diabolo. If the diabolo is not facing the audience properly, by touching it on the edge with a handstick you can make it turn. Experiment with the right place to touch your diabolo to make it turn back to the center.

Figure 8.21   Catch the diabolo on crossed handsticks for a dramatic finale.

95 • *Passing With a Partner*

With two or more players you can pass the diabolo from string to string. You can toss it from side to side (figure 8.22) or from front to back and it will be spinning in the correct direction for your partner to catch and continue. If you toss it front to front, you will need to learn to continue to spin the diabolo the way it is spinning when it lands, which may mean pulling left handed instead of right handed.

Figure 8.22   Passing the diabolo to a partner.

96 ● *Around the World*

Start by building up your RPMs. Once the diabolo is spinning rapidly, swing it in a big arc, as shown in figure 8.23. The diabolo will circle over your head, and you end up with a crossed string. Reverse the process to un-cross the string, or you can turn a pirouette while the diabolo makes its arc. When you are facing front again, the string will not be crossed. Another possibility is that once your strings are crossed, you can cross your arms and push your hands far apart while crossed; the diabolo will fly up off the tightened string. While it is in the air, uncross your arms and catch it back on the tight string, then relax.

Another method of completing around the world with uncrossed strings is to actually circle twice in a row without stopping. The first

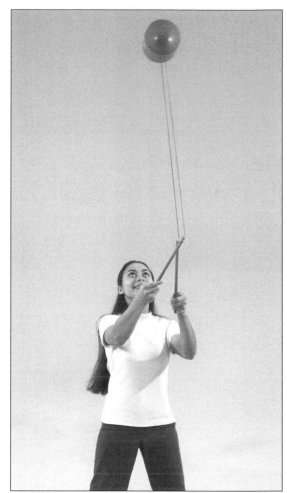

Figure 8.23 Take the diabolo "around the world" by swinging it in a big arc over your head.

swing goes behind your back and the second swing goes in front. You can also do this while facing to the side, and the diabolo will circle first on your right and then on your left.

97 • *Around the World With a Stopover (or Two)*

Swing the diabolo to the right as you did in the previous trick, but stop the string by pushing down on it with your right handstick (figure 8.24a). The diabolo swings up and over the right handstick (figure 8.24b) and comes to rest, still spinning, on the outstretched string. Catch the still-spinning diabolo on the collected strings, as shown in figure 8.24c. To unwrap, reverse the instructions.

Figure 8.24   Around the world with a stopover.

98 • *Two Diabolos on One String*

When using two diabolos on one string, your left hand tosses the diabolos over each other, and your right hand controls the spinning and tilt of both diabolos. To begin, start one diabolo spinning on your string with right-hand pulls. Station a partner to your left. Your partner tosses the second diabolo either from his own string or from his hand with a snap of the wrist so that it is spinning in the same direction as the one on the string (figure 8.25a). The incoming diabolo hits the string midway between the spinning diabolo and the tip of your right handstick. The impact of that incoming diabolo makes the diabolo on the string hop over the one that just landed (figure 8.25b). To keep the diabolos circling around each other, point your handsticks in and use your left hand to toss every time a diabolo comes to your left side (figure 8.25c). The right hand keeps pulling with small upward circles.

Oriental art forms like diabolo and devil stick have recently been developed far beyond their Asian roots, thanks to European and North American players. Thanks to innovations in materials and design, the possibilities are limitless with these fascinating ancient "toys." Although they have been around for thousands of years, new tricks are invented every year, so why not try your hand at these props and add your "spin" to the developing repertoire of exciting moves.

Figure 8.25   *(a)* Dave tosses the white diabolo to Ben,

(continued)

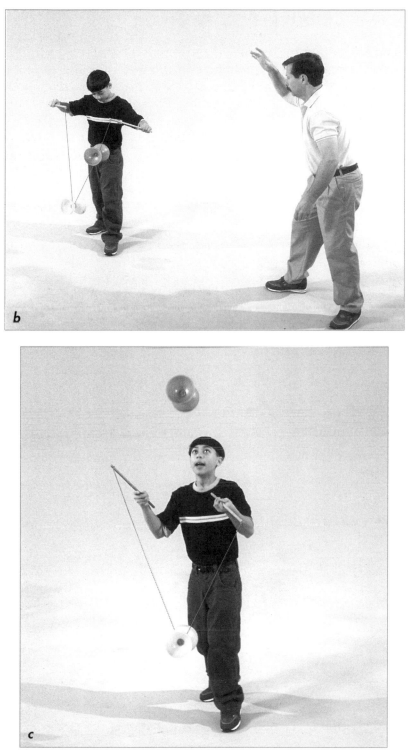

Figure 8.25 *(continued)* and *(b)* Ben catches it and circles the two diabolos on one string or *(c)* tosses them high one by one.

chapter

9

Plate and Ball Spinning

Spinning and balancing have long been associated with juggling. In this chapter we will explore two props that can be used to add these novel skills to your routine and can even be combined with toss juggling for that all-important grand finale.

Plate Spinning

Before the advent of plastic juggling props, jugglers spun real china plates by drilling a shallow hole in the exact center and driving a finishing nail into the end of a stick. Sticks could be stuck into holes on a table to spin multiple plates. The aluminum plate with a cone-shaped center came next, permitting the plate to be started easily and to spin for a long time. You can find plastic plates designed for spinning in magic, toy, or kite stores or on our Web site.

99 • Start Spinning

There are three ways to start spinning:

1. Put the point of the stick in the center of the plate, hold the stick straight up, and pinch the rim of the plate between your thumb and fingertip (figure 9.1a). Pull gently on the edge of the plate to get it started (figure 9.1b). Spin the plate toward yourself. A right-hand plate spins counterclockwise when seen from above.

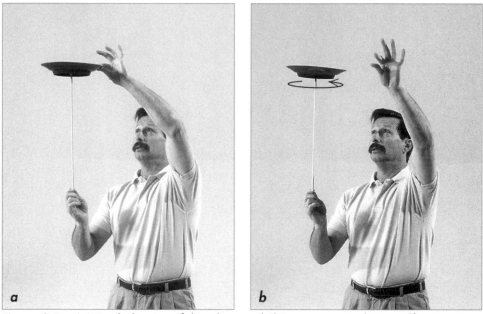

a   b

Figure 9.1   (a) Pinch the rim of the plate and (b) spin it toward yourself.

2. Hold the plate with one hand by the base (figure 9.2a) or with two hands by the rim and toss it into the air, as shown in figure 9.2b. Poke your stick up into the center of the plate as it begins to fall, and cushion the catch.

3. First learn to turn the stick without a plate. Balance the stick with the point up and the flat of the stick in the flat of your palm. Point your index finger up along the stick, not your thumb. Start by making small circles in the air, about six inches in diameter, with your stick. Your wrist should be doing much of the turning. The base of the stick actually rotates so that you can feel it "tickling" your palm.

Figure 9.2 *(a)* Hold the plate with one hand, then *(b)* toss it into the air and catch it with your stick.

Next let the plate hang on the stick by the rim of the base (figure 9.3a). Start turning the stick in the air as described. The plate should stay in one place while the stick turns inside the base. If the stick is held too tightly, the plate will lop around the frozen stick. Loosen your grip on the stick so that it can move freely within the base of the plate. See figure 9.3b.

Once the plate is actually turning, accelerate it by turning faster, as if you are whipping cream. Once it is going around quickly, freeze your hand and wrist and point the stick into the center of the rapidly spinning plate (figure 9.3c). The plate should balance on the stick.

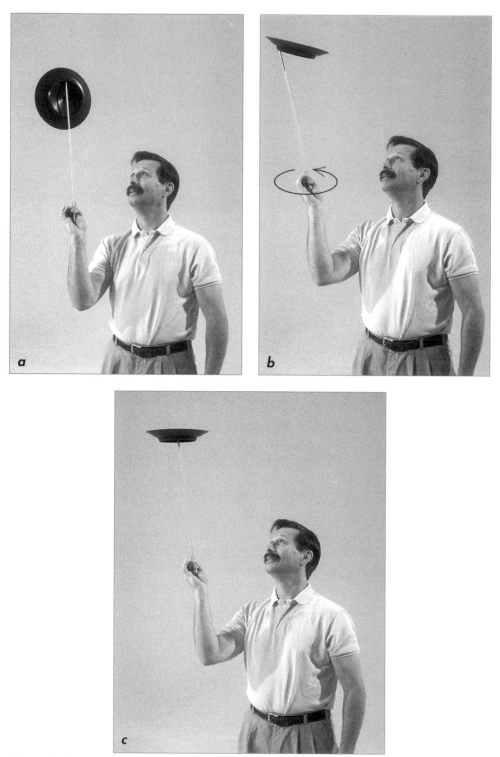

Figure 9.3 *(a)* Let the plate hang on the stick; *(b)* start turning the stick using your wrist; *(c)* freeze your wrist and the plate will balance in the center.

100 • *Throws and Catches*

Start the plate spinning. Toss the plate up from the stick as shown in figure 9.4, and catch it on the same end or on the opposite end of your stick. Toss behind your back or under your leg, or throw the plate up, turn a pirouette, and catch it back on the stick. Hold a stick in each hand and toss the plate back and forth from hand to hand.

Figure 9.4   Toss the plate up and catch it back on the stick.

101 • *Pass Under the Leg*

Get the plate started. Hold onto the stick at a point just a few inches away from the plate. Raise your knee and pass it under, as shown in figure 9.5. For extra points, when the plate comes out from under your leg, why not toss it, pull the stick out from under your leg, and catch the plate back on the stick. You can do this same move with the plate on your upraised finger instead of the stick.

Figure 9.5 Show off your skill and coordination by passing the plate under your leg.

102 • *Curls*

Start the plate spinning. Position your hand on the stick about one foot from the plate. The objective is to bring the plate under your arm and back to the starting position in one smooth move without repositioning your fingers while the plate is en route. Turn your palm up and out and point your index finger down the stick toward the ground (figure 9.6a). After the plate goes under your elbow, raise the stick and circle the bottom of the stick over your shoulder (figure 9.6b), then lower your hand back down to the starting position, as shown in figure 9.6c.

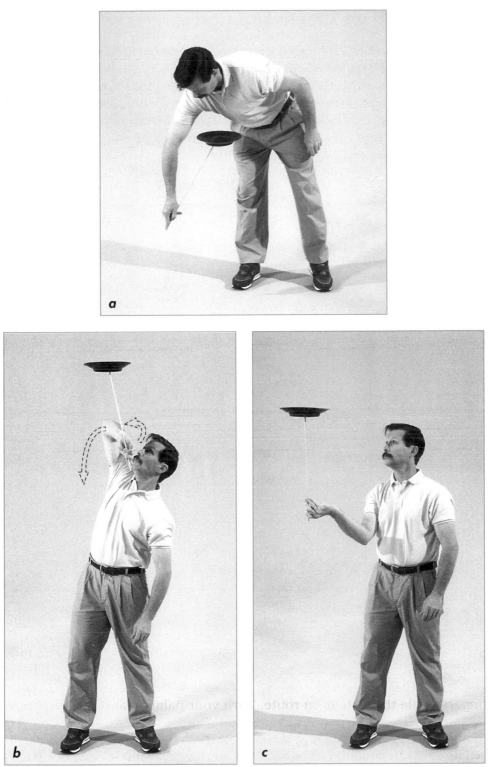

Figure 9.6 The curl should be one smooth move from start to finish.

103 • *Spin on Finger and Curl*

Start the plate on the stick, pass it to your extended middle or index finger, and lower the plate under your arm (figure 9.7a). With your palm always up, your hand spirals under your upper arm, out to the point where your elbow is at its highest point (figure 9.7b), and your thumb is pointing to the rear. Next, raise your hand and keep slowly spiraling inward up to a point high above your head, as your elbow lowers (figure 9.7c). At this point your palm turns back toward you and your hand comes back down to the starting point.

Figure 9.7 Start the plate on your fingertip, then curl under your arm.

There is some contortion required, but the higher you raise your hand before turning it and dropping your elbow, the easier it is on your wrist. You spiral the plate under your arm and up over your shoulder.

104 • *Pass Behind the Back*

You can do this trick by simply handing the stick across (figure 9.8), from one stick to another, or from one finger to another. After practicing curling or passing a spinning plate under your leg or behind your back, the same moves with a spinning ball will be easier to learn.

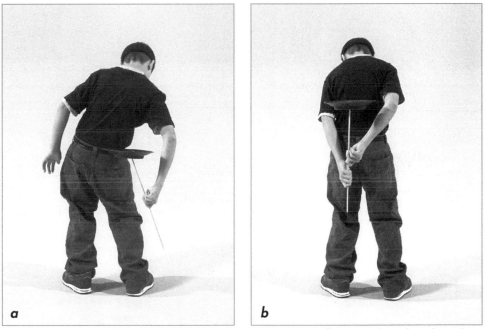

a   b

Figure 9.8   Reach behind your back and pass the stick from one hand to the other.

105 • *Balancing a Spinning Plate*

Once the plate is spinning, put the base of the stick on the palm of your hand or on a fingertip and look at the point where the stick touches the plate (figure 9.9). You will automatically adjust to keep the plate from falling. Try the same balance with the stick on your chin or forehead.

Figure 9.9 Try balancing the spinning plate on your fingertip.

While balancing a plate and stick on the palm of your hand, why not try to juggle two or more balls or rings with the other hand, or four balls or rings. The fact that you are looking up anyway makes this trick easier than it looks. The weight of the plate helps keep the stick from falling.

106 • *Spinning Multiple Plates*

You can start up to four plates, one at a time, with one hand and hold them in the other hand once they are spinning. Just hold one stick between every two fingers. The hard part is keeping the plates from bumping into each other. The longer the sticks are, the closer together you can hold them, and the less danger there is of collisions.

107 • *Partner Tricks*

You can hand or toss a plate to your partner, from your stick to hers. You can each start a plate spinning on a stick. Just decide who will toss high and who will toss low. See figure 9.10.

Figure 9.10   Passing plates.

Ball Spinning

The best ball for learning to spin is the large Slo-Mo ball from Jugglebug, available from our Web site or at most magic, kite, and independent toy stores. Fill it so that it will dimple at the bottom when you put it on your finger. Once you can spin a Slo-Mo ball, try other balls, such as soccer or playground balls that are smaller and more fully inflated. They may be more difficult to start and to balance, but they can be spun much longer, especially if the surface is smooth and untextured. Jugglers generally turn spinning balls inward in order to permit them to be curled easily, whereas basketball players generally turn spinning balls outward, permitting them to be accelerated by brushing with the fingertips away from the face.

108 ◦ *One-Handed Start*

Hold the ball on your fingertips, as shown in figure 9.11a. Twist your arm so that you are looking at the back of your hand. Throw and spin at the same time (figure 9.11b). Give as much momentum to the ball as possible, but just toss it a few inches high. Catch by absorbing the shock slightly. Keep your index finger straight and your other fingers tucked in tightly (figure 9.11c).

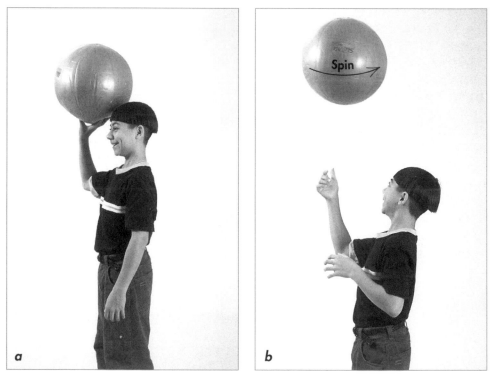

Figure 9.11 *(a)* Hold the ball with one hand, *(b)* spin,

(continued)

c

Figure 9.11   *(continued)* and *(c)* catch.

109 ● *Two-Handed Start*

To get more initial RPMs, hold your right hand directly in front of your face, palm out, and your left hand on the other side of the ball, palm in (figure 9.12a). To spin, pull sharply out with both hands, leaving your fingers in contact with the ball for as long as possible. Throw about one foot high, as straight up as possible (figure 9.12b). Catch on your extended finger (figure 9.12c). Finding the "South Pole" on the ball comes with practice.

a

Figure 9.12   *(a)* Hold the ball with two hands,
(continued)

Figure 9.12 *(continued)* then *(b)* spin, and *(c)* catch.

110 • *Maintaining the Spin*

Many ball spinners use the back of the fingernail to maintain the spin for a longer duration. However, if the ball is full and has a slick surface, it may be easier to balance on the pad of the finger or the fingertip. Imagine a rod running through your finger and the ball. Keep this rod straight up and down and your finger rigid. Look at the top of the ball. If you cannot see the top, focus on the point where the rod would protrude from the top. To keep the ball spinning longer, brush the ball lightly with your free hand, contacting the ball at or below

Figure 9.13 To keep the ball spinning, brush it toward you lightly with your free hand.

the equator (figure 9.13). If you practice a great deal, you may be able to use the tip of your middle finger to give a delicate push to the ball.

111 • *Curls*

A spinning ball naturally migrates in the direction of spin. If you spin a ball with your right hand toward the outside (or clockwise when seen from the top) and then try to curl it under your arm, you fight the natural inclination of the spinning ball, and it will fall easily. However, if a right-hand ball is spinning counterclockwise when you curl it under your arm, it is moving naturally in the appropriate direction. Keep your palm up through the entire process. Bend sideways at the waist to give the ball enough room to pass under your upper arm (figure 9.14a). Once your elbow is pointing up, straighten and raise your arm as high as possible, lowering your elbow while turning your palm away from you (figure 9.14b). Finally, your hand comes back down to the original position as your palm turns back in to face you again, as shown in figure 9.14c. Practice with a plate first to master the contortion required.

Figure 9.14   Curls: *(a)* start, *(b)* mid-position,

(continued)

Figure 9.14   *(continued)* and *(c)* finish.

112 ● *Passing a Spinning Ball*

While the ball is spinning, you can pass it under your leg and pop it up on the other side. Put your leg back down and catch the ball on your finger again. You can also transfer a ball from hand to hand in front or even behind your back.

113 ● *Chest Roll*

Hold the ball in one hand with your arm extended. Start with a nudge from your fingertips (figure 9.15a). Lean back slightly and keep your chin back. The ball rolls right across your chest and out to your other arm. You can then stop the ball when it gets to your other hand (figure 9.15b) and reverse the direction. The hardest part of this move is the second half, from the chest out to the palm. Practice the first and easiest part. Then practice starting the ball on your chest and pushing it with your right hand toward the left. With an appropriately timed toss you can keep the ball going around and around in one direction by curving your arms toward each other after the ball has gone across your chest and rolling it across the gap between your hands.

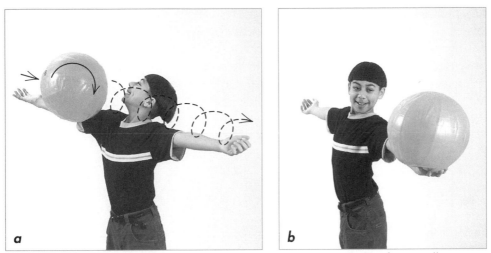

Figure 9.15   *(a)* Use your fingertips to start the ball rolling; *(b)* after it rolls across your chest use your other hand to stop it.

114 • *Back Rolls and Head Rolls*

To roll across your back, try to create a ramp, as shown in figure 9.16. As with the front roll, the second half is the most difficult. With practice you can get the ball to go from the back of one hand and down the arm to the back of the neck; with luck you can stop it there. However, to go out the other arm and catch on the back of the extended hand takes a great deal

Figure 9.16   Create a ramp across your shoulders for the back roll.

of practice. Practice with only a light T-shirt, as the feel of the ball on your arm and shoulders is important. Use a Slo-Mo ball or a basketball so that you have enough texture and weight. Playground balls also work well for this move.

Another popular trick that takes a great deal of practice is the head roll. Start by tossing a ball to your forehead. A gymnastic ball or stage ball works well. Once you can catch the tossed ball on your forehead, learn to balance it there (figure 9.17a). Next, practice balancing the ball on your temple on each side of your head (figure 9.17b). Then learn to toss to your forehead and roll to the temple. Learn to roll from the temple to the forehead. Finally, learn to roll from temple to temple across the forehead. This trick will require many hours of concentrated practice.

Figure 9.17 Roll the ball from *(a)* the forehead to *(b)* the temple.

115 • Spinning Two Balls

Learn to start spinning with each hand. Both balls will be coming in toward you as shown by the arrows in figure 9.18. You must not look at either ball or try to follow it to keep it balanced, but must just keep your fingers straight and let the balls find their natural points of balance. If you can curl a ball under each arm, you can curl successively under both arms. Start by curling the ball that is more difficult for you, usually the one in the nondominant hand. As you bring your hand up behind your back, twist your wrist and lower your elbow. Now it is time to start the other ball under the opposite arm.

Figure 9.18   Double your fun by spinning two balls.

Keep your focus on the ball going under the arm. Try to get both balls under, then toss them from your fingertips to the opposite hands to catch dramatically.

116 • Spinning a Ball on a Ball

Spin the first ball on the fingertip of your dominant hand. Place the second ball on top of the first, right in the center (figure 9.19). Don't give it any spin. After a careful release it will roll around on the first ball. Look at the juncture between the two balls to achieve balance.

Figure 9.19 With lots of practice you can learn to spin a ball on a ball.

*W*hen spinning balls, stay erect and strike vivid poses with arms and legs outstretched. Hold these poses long enough for the audience to see the trick, but not long enough to drop the ball. If you are balancing one ball, your other hand can flourish or point toward the spinning ball for emphasis. Combine ball spinning with one hand and toss juggling with the other for a difficult but crowd-pleasing combination trick.

Spinning plates and balls can add variety to your act. Once you can spin a plate or a ball, you can begin to put combination tricks together. Start your spinning objects first, then juggle with your other hand. A great combination trick doesn't need to last very long, just long enough for the audience to get a mental snapshot. How's this for a goal: While idling on your unicycle, spin a plate on a mouthstick and a ball on the left hand while juggling two rings with the right hand and turning two rings around one leg. It's been done before, so it is possible. Good luck!

chapter 10

Boxes and Hats

In vaudeville days elegant gentleman jugglers could entertain with only three balls, a top hat, a cane, and three cigar boxes. These props still represent style and panache. You don't have to wear a tailcoat, but you may feel justifiably stylish once you master these traditional props.

Boxes

Chinese jugglers traditionally manipulated wooden blocks. They taught the skill to Japanese jugglers who brought it to Europe in the last few decades of the 19th century. W.C. Fields popularized this art in North America, having learned it from a juggler named Harrigan who had learned it in Europe. In vaudeville days jugglers traditionally manipulated cigar boxes reinforced with additional wood inside, with leather glued on the ends. Now, sturdy and highly reinforced wooden, plastic, and foam cigar boxes are made not to hold cigars, but solely for juggling. They can be bought from top magic stores or from a number of prop makers.

One-pound coffee cans, the use of which was invented by eminent Baltimore area juggler Laura Green, are an alternative to cigar boxes. Open one end of each of three cans just enough to empty out the coffee. Put the plastic lid back on and get one for the other end as well. Tape the lids in place and use hot glue to secure felt to the lids. This coffee-can cigar box is very easy to manipulate, and almost all of the tricks explained in this chapter can be executed with these makeshift boxes. If coffee cans are too big, try smaller cans until you find some that are just right for you.

117 • *Releasing and Catching*

Start by holding three boxes at waist height as shown in figure 10.1a. Raise your hands and separate the end boxes (figure 10.1b). Lower your arms, keep your back straight, bend your knees, and catch the middle box (figure 10.1c). Practice until you establish a rhythm. Release high, bend your knees and catch low, rise up, release again, and catch again. This should be a very athletic move, much like deep knee bends.

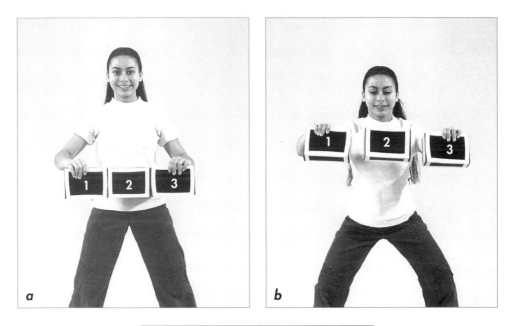

Figure 10.1 *(a)* Hold the boxes at waist level, *(b)* release high, and *(c)* catch low.

118 • *Turning One End*

While going up and down as you learned in the previous move, pull one end box away when your boxes are at chest height, turn the box 90 degrees, and trap the middle box when you are at the bottom of a shallow knee bend (figure 10.2a). Learn to turn that box 180 degrees, as shown in figure 10.2b, and then work on the other hand.

Figure 10.2   Try turning the end box *(a)* 90 degrees, then *(b)* 180 degrees.

119 • *Turning Both Ends*

Raise your hands slightly and separate both end boxes. Now you can trap the middle box with both palms in (figure 10.3), or with both palms up (figure 10.4). You can alternate, turning and trapping with the right, turning and trapping with the left, as shown in figure 10.5. Work constantly on that up-and-down rhythm.

Figure 10.3 Trapping the middle box with both palms in.

Figure 10.4 Trapping the middle box with both palms up.

Figure 10.5 Alternating, with one palm up and one down.

120 • *Take Out and Pull Down*

Start with the boxes at waist height, as shown in figure 10.6a. Release the right box and grab the middle box straight down with your right hand (figure 10.6b). Scoop the middle box under the right box (figure 10.6c) and trap the right box in the middle, as in figure 10.6d. None of the boxes tumbles or turns in this move. Now learn to do this on the other side and practice until you can do each side in turn over and over again using the rhythm you worked on in skill 119.

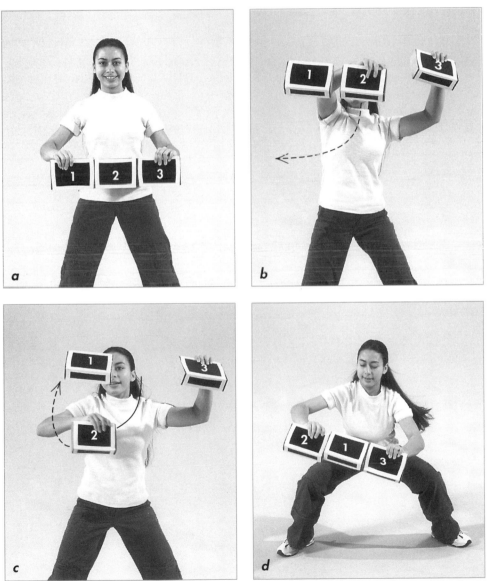

Figure 10.6   *(a)* Start with the boxes at waist height; *(b)* grab the middle box; *(c)* scoop it under the right box; and *(d)* trap the right box in the middle.

121 • *Take Out and Pull Up*

Release the right box, grab the middle box, and pull up. Arc the middle box over the right box and trap the right box in the middle. None of the boxes tumbles or turns in this move. You'll need to bend lower than in skill 120 to make this catch because the boxes are falling while you are first pulling up and then down. Now learn the other side. Learn to pull up left and then right in succession.

122 • *Spinning the Middle Box*

As you raise your hands, release the middle box as you did in skill 117, but toss the middle box a bit in the air using the ends of the other two boxes. With practice you can spin the middle box so that it turns toward the right or toward the left, a quarter turn, a half turn, or all the way around, before you trap it again. You can learn to spin the middle box in any of three planes, as shown in figure 10.7, and in either direction. This move will help you make saves later when you are trying more complicated tricks.

Figure 10.7 When you release the middle box, spin it 90, 180, or 360 degrees then trap it again.

123 • *Under the Leg*

Swing your boxes to one side, separate the end boxes, and put your leg through the gap, trapping the middle box again under your upraised knee, as shown in figure 10.8. You can balance on this leg for a while for comic effect, or you can reverse the process, make a gap, and bring your leg back out immediately.

Figure 10.8 Trapping the middle box under your leg is an impressive move.

124 • *Behind the Back*

Try the same move with your entire body. Separate one end box while swinging your arms toward the back, move through the gap and trap the middle box behind your back (figure 10.9). You can create a gap again, while the boxes are behind your back, and step back through the gap. Another way to get the boxes from back to front is to use the two end boxes to pitch the middle box between your legs, catching it in front again.

Figure 10.9 Trapping the middle box behind your back requires quickness and a lot of practice!

125 • *Trapping Your Knee, Hip, or Head*

For comedic effect, and to take a breather while executing a strenuous box routine, you can pretend you are trying to trap the middle box, but trap your knee (figure 10.10a), waist, or head (figure 10.10b).

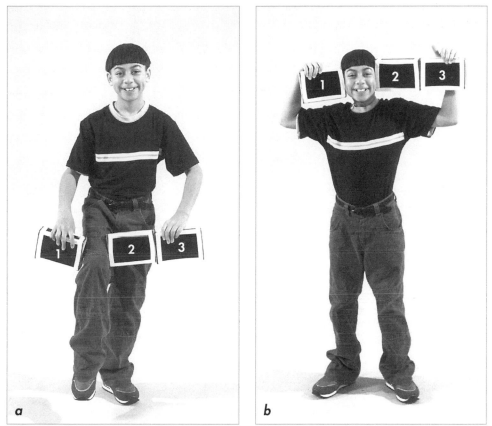

Figure 10.10 To give your audience a laugh, trap *(a)* your knee or *(b)* your head.

126 • *Vertical Tricks*

Start in the "home" position, with the boxes aligned, and raise one end high. Take your hand off the topmost box, grab the middle box, and push it out (figure 10.11a). This will cause the top box to tumble down toward the lower box. Bend your knees slightly to absorb the shock of the falling box and trap it between the other two (figure 10.11b).

Pull out the top and bottom boxes, bring them back in, and trap the middle box. Now turn that stack on end, tumble out the middle box, and trap again.

Figure 10.11   *(a)* Push the center box out, causing the top box to tumble; *(b)* trap the tumbling box in the center.

Of course, you can add drama by balancing three stacked boxes. Looking at the top box, balance the stack on one finger. Try spinning the tower of balanced boxes on that one finger. Now balance the stack of three on your chin.

127 • Release and Regrasp Tricks

Pull all three boxes straight up to your chest. Release them all, as shown in figure 10.12, and regrasp as low as you can. Let them fall to about your knees before you catch them again. While they are in the air you can clap, slap your cheeks, or turn a pirouette, then grasp them again just at the last moment.

While the boxes are together in the air, you can tumble them toward you or cross your arms to catch.

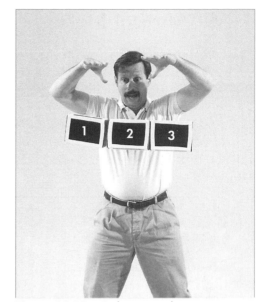

Figure 10.12   Release and regrasp.

128 • Crossing and Uncrossing Your Arms

You can separate an end box, #3, pulling it down and under the entire line of boxes. Then release the box on the other end, #1, with your other hand and regrasp the box that was in the center, #2, with this empty hand, ending up with your arms crossed (figure 10.13). To uncross, lift the two end boxes (releasing the middle box), open your arms toward the outside, and regrasp the middle box.

Figure 10.13   Catch with crossed arms.

129 • *Clap and Trap*

You can separate both end boxes and clap them over the middle box in the air, then trap the middle box again (figure 10.14 a-c). For extra points separate and clap both above and below the falling box before trapping the middle box again.

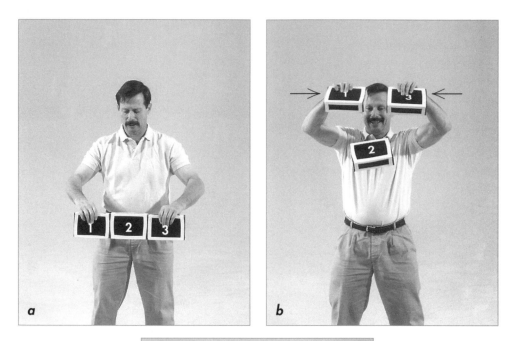

Figure 10.14 *(a)* Start with the boxes at waist height, *(b)* clap the two end boxes together, then *(c)* trap the middle box again.

130 ● *Pass Across*

This is a fast move. Raise all three boxes above chest height, separate and lift one box, #3, off the end (figure 10.15), pass this box to your other hand, regrasp #2 with the passing hand, and trap the middle box, #1, with both end boxes before they hit the ground. Practice in both directions. See if you can send one box back and forth across the top of the line of boxes.

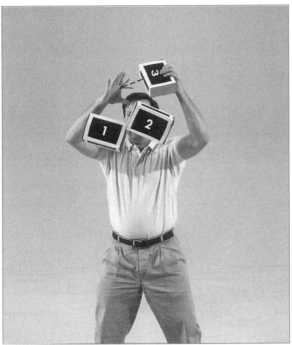

Figure 10.15   Pass the box across to the other hand then trap the middle box, which is #1.

Hats

Hat manipulation can be a show-stopper with plenty of comic moments and surprises for your audience. Any all-felt topper or derby will do, although a heavy hat is better than a light one. You will break your hat in as you practice. It starts out stiff and ends up floppy and soft. Getting the hat wet will shrink and round out the top of a flat topper, so if you want to keep the shape, avoid wearing it out in the rain. If you need to stiffen the brim for certain tricks, use sizing, available in the same location as laundry starch in grocery stores. Get a hat that is at least one-eighth size too big so that you can catch it easily on your head. Avoid the old-style top hats with cardboard stiffening, as they will get broken and beat up in very short order. Check our Web site for traditional felt toppers.

131 • *Rolling Down the Arm*

To take your hat off, tap it upward with a finger at the back, and aim it down your outstretched arm, palm up (figure 10.16a). The front of the brim will touch your shoulder, the leading edge of the crown will touch your elbow, the trailing edge of the crown will hit just above the wrist (figure 10.16b), and you should catch the hat by the brim, crown up, as shown in figure 10.16c.

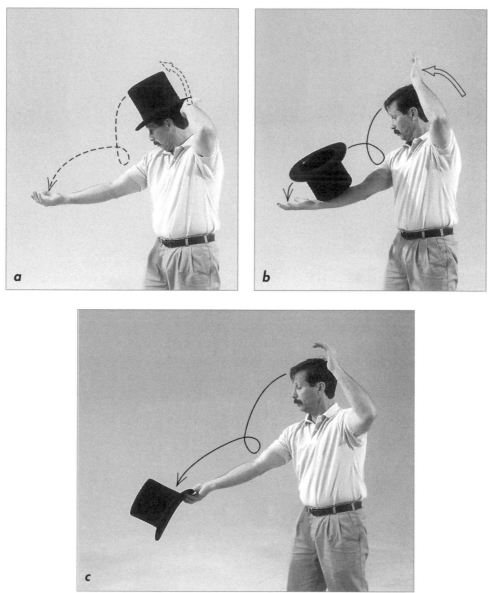

Figure 10.16 To roll the hat down your arm, *(a)* tap it upward with your finger, *(b)* watch it roll down your outstretched arm, and *(c)* catch it by the brim.

132 • *Replacing on the Head*

To get the hat back on your head from the final position in the last move, flop the crown over your thumb and back past your wrist (figure 10.17a). Raise your arm at the shoulder, raise your elbow, and place the hat on your head with your hand at the back of the brim (figure 10.17b). Your thumb is on top of the brim, and your fingers are all pointing in toward your back and downward.

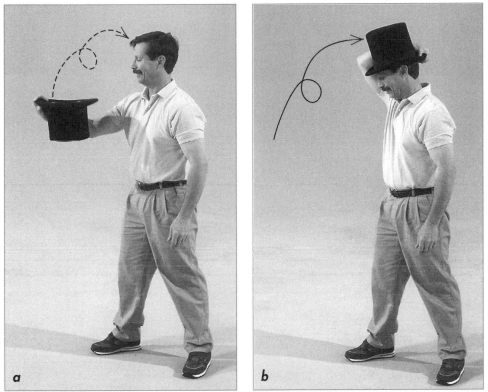

Figure 10.17   To place it back on your head, *(a)* flip the hat to the position shown, and *(b)* bend your arm to bring the hat up to your head.

133 • *Rolling to the Head*

A more difficult method of replacing the hat is to roll it back on the top of your arm following the steps for rolling down your arm, but in reverse order. Use your upper arm to guide the hat onto your forehead, as shown in figure 10.18. Start with your arm outstretched and your hand held higher than your forehead. Let gravity assist, but the initial flop onto the crown and the nudge you give the hat must be precise, or you'll overshoot your head. The higher the crown, the harder this move is.

Figure 10.18   *(a)* Use your upper arm to guide the hat to your forehead, and *(b)* voila!

134 ● *Turning Off and Back On*

This method of removal and return is foolproof, as you never let go of the hat. Put both hands up with elbows out, your thumbs on top of the brim, and fingers beneath it (figure 10.19a). Rotate your wrists forward. Once the crown is down (figure 10.19b), you can roll the hat once or twice more by turning the brim over your fingers like a baton. To return the hat to your head, just reverse the process. Start with your thumbs on top of the brim and roll it back up.

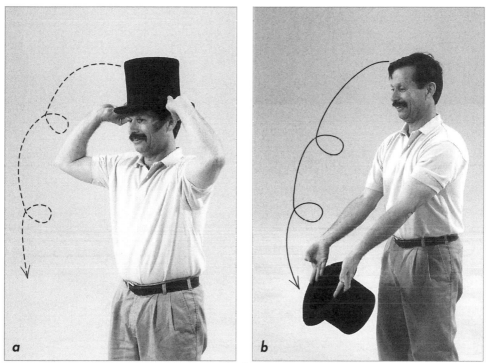

Figure 10.19   *(a)* Use both hands to *(b)* flip the hat off, then reverse the process to put it back on.

135 • *Flipping Your Lid*

Hold the hat on your right side with your right hand. Your thumb is on top of the brim, and all your fingers are spread out under the brim (figure 10.20a). Flip it by tossing up and to the left so that the brim rotates around the crown (figure 10.20b). Catch with the left hand on the left side, with your thumb over the brim and your fingers beneath it (figure 10.20c). Toss it back and forth. Try single and double flips. For comic effect practice reaching out to catch as if the hat were trying to escape.

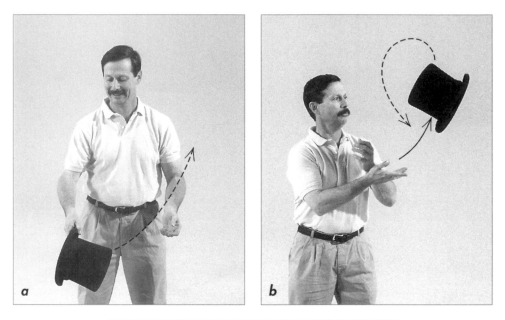

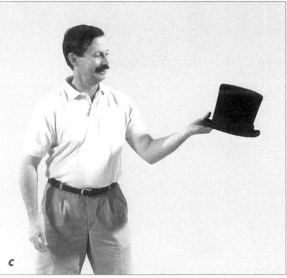

Figure 10.20 Flipping your hat from side to side: *(a)* start, *(b)* flip, and *(c)* catch.

136 • *Flopping Your Lid*

Hold the hat with your fingers inside the hat and your thumb on top of the brim. If you are holding the hat in your right hand, the crown should point to the left, as shown in figure 10.21a. Flop the hat over your thumb so that the brim is around your thumb and the crown is pointing down. (Note: When you first practice, you can pause at this point. Eventually eliminate the pause to make the move more flowing.) Let go of the brim (figure 10.21b); as the hat begins to fall, turn your wrist quickly and catch by the crown, with your thumb back in the original position and your fingers inside the hat again (figure 10.21c).

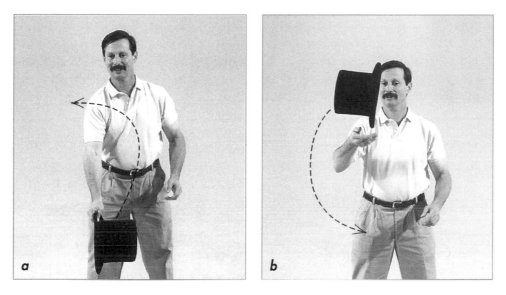

Figure 10.21   Flopping your hat to the left: *(a)* start, *(b)* flop, and *(c)* catch.

Needless to say, you can execute a series of flops, first in one direction with one hand, then flip your hat across and go in the other direction with the other hand. You can also flop toward the front, directly at the front row of the audience. For maximum effect, take more time than is necessary to turn your wrist and catch, and reach way out to get the hat, just before it hits a spectator. Don't worry about misses. It's just a hat.

137 • *Tumbling Your Hat*

The tumble can be started with the crown toward you or away from you. Place your right hand on top of the crown and your left hand on the bottom. Both hands are palm down to start so that the hat is trapped between the palm of the right hand on top and the back of the left hand below (figure 10.22a). The controlling hand is now the right because it is the one on top. The right palm stays in toward the hat until the left hand gets to the top, rotates palm downward, and takes control (figure 10.22b). At this point the right hand is on the bottom, it rotates, and the hat is trapped between the back of the right hand and the palm of the left. Your hands rotate in a twiddling motion around and around each other, and the hat tumbles, rolling around each wrist in turn. Whenever the hand on the bottom turns, it slides inward, toward the brim.

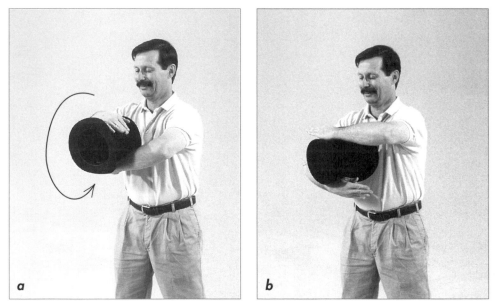

Figure 10.22 Tumbling your hat around each wrist.

138 • *Balancing Your Hat*

You can balance your hat anywhere on your body as long as you can see the uppermost part of the brim. It is easier to balance if the brim is stiff, so once you have broken in your hat, you may need to use starch or sizing to stiffen the brim. Inquire at a hat store for the best procedure. Try balancing on your hand, your foot, and your nose. To balance the hat on your nose, tilt your head back and look up (figure 10.23). Focus on the center of the sweat band. Keep your movements small and precise. Drop your chin forward and with practice you can make the hat plop down on your head.

Figure 10.23 Balancing the hat on your nose.

139 • *Toss to the Head*

Hold your hat crown up with your thumb on top of the brim and your fingers inside. Toss and, at the last minute, duck your head under the hat. Gradually work on the accuracy of your flip until you can toss it to your head without ducking. Once you can toss with a single flip to your head, learn a double flip.

140 • *Toss to the Hand (Over the Head)*

After you have learned to toss the hat to your head, you can surprise the audience by tossing it once or twice to your head, and then toss it up as if it is going to your head, but instead reach high up over your head and catch the rim of the hat without looking (figure 10.24). The trick is, of course, to practice the move until it is automatic. You catch with your hand in a C shape, thumb down. The brim should insert right into the C of your cupped hand, and you simply clamp down on it. When you first practice, you will bend your elbow, but eventually learn to toss higher and catch with your arm stretched out. Lower the hat to your head and look surprised.

Figure 10.24 Toss the hat to your hand without looking.

141 • *Roll Down the Back and Up Again*

Roll the hat down your back by tipping your head back. You may need to nudge it off your head with a touch of one hand. Put both hands behind your back and catch it blind at waist level with the crown up (figure 10.25a). Bend forward at a 45-degree angle and use both hands to roll the hat back up (figure 10.25b). Before letting go of the hat to roll it up your back, you will need to raise your hands at least a few inches higher than the point at which you caught it. Eventually this point becomes a habit, and you will always roll the hat from this exact point and with the exact force needed to get it up to your head. The hat teeters on your neck and plops onto your head.

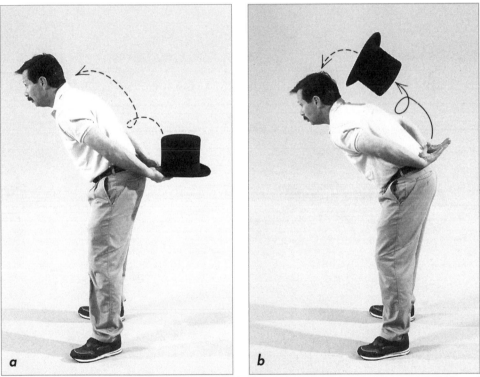

Figure 10.25 To roll the hat up your back, *(a)* start with the crown up, and *(b)* bend forward and use both hands to roll it upward.

With a bit of mime and a little imagination, your hat can become a steering wheel with a horn in the center, or a Frisbee. You can place the hat on the floor and get into it with a front roll or a back bend. You can catch objects in the brim or on the crown of your hat. Your entire act can appear out of your hat. Your hat can be used to pick a volunteer or to make an audience member look special for that "Kodak Moment."

142 • *Roll on the Brim*

Hold the hat either with the crown toward or away from the audience. Toss it up and spin it like a ring or a Frisbee so that it turns in the direction you want it to roll. Make a ramp across your back and down at a slight angle. Let the hat roll down your arm (figure 10.26a), across your shoulders, and out to your other hand. Catch the hat with the thumb on the top and your fingers under the brim (figure 10.26b). Once you can roll in one direction, try the other. If the crown is toward the front, you really need to duck your head forward as it comes over your shoulders to avoid hitting the back of your head.

Figure 10.26 Toss the hat up and spin it, then let it roll (a) across your arm and (b) out to your other hand.

143 • *Toss Under the Arm*

Using the flip you have practiced to toss your hat to your head, you can toss the hat behind your back and under your other arm (figure 10.27 a-c). You can even toss under a leg, let it flip once or twice, and catch it on your head. The key is to look up until the very last second and then duck under the hat.

Figure 10.27   *(a)* Toss the hat behind your back, *(b)* under your arm, and *(c)* let it plop onto your head.

144 • *Kick Up*

There are at least three ways to get your hat to your foot. You can toss it from your hand with a single flip, you can tip it off your head by nudging it up at the back so that it falls off and to the front, or you can pick up a dropped hat by sticking your foot under the brim. Once the hat is on your foot, readjust it by jiggling your foot so that it balances on the end of your toe with a single point of contact on the sweat band. Flip it back up to your head with a high kick, as shown in figure 10.28. Look up and duck under at the last moment to catch it on your head.

Figure 10.28   Flip the hat to your head with a high kick.

145 • *Spinning Your Hat*

Hold your hat with your thumb under the brim and the hat hanging vertically (figure 10.29a). Your elbow should be straight. Bend your elbow as you lift and spin the hat around your extended fingers (figure 10.29b). As it finishes its spin, reinsert your thumb and grasp it again. Lift, spin and let go, extend your arm, and regrasp, over and over.

This same move can be done as a flourish, with the hat held over the head, spinning it around your extended fingers. Push it up, spin, and regrasp.

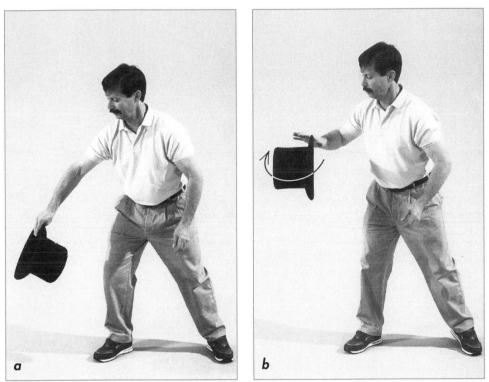

Figure 10.29   *(a)* Hold the hat so it hangs vertically, then *(b)* lift and spin the hat around your extended fingers.

146 • *Toss to a Fist or Hat Rack*

Hold your hat with the open brim pointed at your target, your thumb on top of the brim and your fingers inside the hat. Stand about six to eight feet away. Eventually you will know just how far away to stand. Toss directly at an outstretched arm, a hat rack (figure 10.30), or your partner's head. Practice tossing the hat back and forth with your partner to develop this skill.

Figure 10.30   *(a)* Point the open brim toward the hat rack, *(b)* throw,

(continued)

Figure 10.30 *(continued)* and (c) ta-da!

Interactive hat manipulation between two or more jugglers is a great crowd-pleaser. You can use the hat as an additional prop in your passing pattern, in place of a ball or club. You and your partner can use the hat to spice up a run-around, stealing the hat before you steal the balls or clubs.

147 ⚬ *Juggling Three Hats*

Start by learning the move with one hand and two hats. Learn it on each side, then put both sides together. Put one hat on your head and hold the other in your hand ready to toss onto your head with a single flip. Throw the hat from your hand, and with the same motion, reach up and remove the hat from your head with that same hand. Take the hat off with your fingers under the brim and your thumb on top. Catch the thrown hat on your head. Repeat. Now try it on the other side until either hand can toss a hat perfectly to your head and remove the one that is there. Once you can do this on both sides, put a hat in each hand and a third hat on your head. Now simply alternate, right-hand throw, remove, catch on head, left-hand throw, remove, catch on head.

148 • *Passing the Hat*

This may be the most important move to learn in the entire book. It is certainly your most dangerous trick. If done incorrectly, you turn into a magician and the entire audience disappears.

Steps in hat passing include:

The First Warning—When people have settled in for your show, and you have won them over with your skill and charm, let them know that at the end of the show you will be passing the hat. Do this right after a joke; while they are laughing, say something like, "By the way, at the end of this show I will be passing my hat!" Pause for two beats and say with a smile, "You're not laughing anymore!"

The Final Warning—Just before your spectacular finale, tell the assembled throng that you will pass the hat after the next trick. Smile and say something like, "After this trick I'm going to be passing my hat, so all the cheapskates can leave now!"

The Request—Just after you have successfully completed that spectacular trick, and while you still have everyone's attention, take off your hat with a flourish, pull out a five-dollar bill, and let the audience know that "this is the average donation, although some generous fans do give more." It helps to have a confederate in the back, "bottling" the crowd with a second hat.

The Pass—Keep talking. "That's it, folks, don't be bashful. It's just like church. Give today so you won't feel guilty tomorrow. I've done my part; the rest is up to you." Look each donor in the eye, smile, and thank him or her profusely. Don't forget to have business cards ready to give out to prospects who might want to hire you.

Boxes and hats can become a strong "signature" routine marking you as a true professional of the old school. Your hat will become your best friend, especially if you pass it at the end of your act. There is no doubt when you appear with your hat that something special is going to happen.

chapter

11

Juggling Games

Jugglers are generally playful people. There are a number of group juggling games that are challenging and fun. Some are competitive; others are simply so frenetic that there are no winners and losers, just players who are 100 percent engaged 100 percent of the time as they get a good aerobic workout.

149 • Circle Games With Scarves

Players form a circle and face inward. Everyone has one scarf. When the leader says, "throw and go," everyone tosses the scarf straight up and high in the air, takes a step to the right, and catches the scarf of the person to the right. Get a rhythm going as you move to the right around the circle: "throw and go, throw and go, throw and go." At some point immediately after everyone has caught a scarf, the leader says, "To the left! Throw and go, throw and go, throw and go," and players reverse the direction of the circle.

You can do the same move faced to the right so that you are facing the back of the juggler in front of you. When the leader says "throw and go," everyone tosses straight up and steps forward to catch the scarf of the person in front. The leader may say, "other way," at which point players turn around and go in the opposite direction.

Keep a pile of extra scarves in the center of the circle so that those who lose a scarf can dive in and get a spare. Once you can do this with one scarf, try it with two apiece. A variation is to toss the scarves to the person to the right, but not to move around the circle. Scarves move; people stay still.

150 • *Relay Races With Scarves*

Form lines of about six jugglers each. Lines don't have to be even. Each person has two scarves. The person in front is the line leader. When the leaders say "throw and go," everyone tosses two scarves straight up and steps forward to catch the scarves in the air. The line leader must run to the back and catch the scarves tossed by the last person in line. See which team can keep going the longest without letting the pattern fall apart, or challenge each team to bring the leader back to the front of the line five times.

151 • *Group Juggling With Beanbags*

This is a great mixer or ice-breaker for a group with up to 25 nonjugglers. Have players form a circle, facing inward. Place a bucket or box of beanbags or JuggleBeanBalls next to you on your throwing side. Tell everyone to put their hands out in front in the catching position. Look at someone across the circle and ask them for their first name. Repeat their name and toss a ball to them. Tell them to make eye contact with someone across from them and ask their name. They repeat the name and toss the beanbag across to that person. Explain that as soon as players have caught and thrown one beanbag, they must put their hands behind their backs. Also, tell everyone to remember the name of the person who threw to them and of the person to whom they threw.

   Once you have been all the way around the circle, and everyone's hands are behind their backs, the last person tosses the ball to you. Now the fun begins. Ask everyone to bring their hands to the front again and point to the person from whom they received a ball and then to the person to whom they will be throwing. Tell them that they will need to always follow that path, and to only throw after they have said the name and gotten the attention of their intended receiver. Tell them not to worry about dropped balls, but to just focus on the next catch. Start slowly by tossing balls one by one across to the person to whom you initially threw, calling their name and getting their attention each time. Balls start flying faster and faster, and everyone is soon calling out names. Go until pandemonium levels are high, then push your bucket out into the middle of the circle and tell everyone to return their balls to the container. By the time this game is over, everyone will be howling with laughter, and they will certainly know many of the names of the group members.

152 • *Joggling*

Joggling, which involves juggling and running at the same time, is fast becoming an acknowledged sport, and races are held annually at the IJA festival. You can use beanbags, balls, or clubs. The penalty for a drop is the loss of time it takes to stop, pick up the object, and continue juggling and running from where the drop occurred. If you are a runner, why not combine the two activities and start recording your times.

153 • *Obstacle Relay Race*

Each team is in a straight line with one person behind the other; the front person is holding three beanbags. Walk the course for the assembled competitors so that they can see what is expected of them. Obstacles may include kneeling down and crawling, climbing over an obstacle, sitting on a chair, walking backward, weaving around traffic cones, or any other obstacles you can invent, all to be navigated while juggling continuously. When the starter says "Go!" the first person from each team runs and juggles through the obstacles, returning to their line and passing the three beanbags to the next person in line. Continue until the last person has run the course. Cheer everyone across the line.

154 • *Hot Potato*

Players stand in a circle facing inward. Each player holds two balls. One player starts juggling with three balls, one of which is unique enough that it can be readily identified. In fact, you can use a real potato as the "odd ball." That hot potato is passed from juggler to juggler. You must toss it high enough that it could be caught, and the recipient must catch it into a juggle. The object is to "fake out" the other players, but not drop the ball yourself. Have players who miss step back until only one remains.

155 • *J-U-G-G-L-E-R*

This game is played like H-O-R-S-E in basketball. One person executes a juggling move and the other people in the game must execute the same move. Every time you miss, you get a letter in the word *juggler*. When you get all seven letters, you are out. The last one out is the winner.

156 • Jollyball

Jollyball is a combination of juggling and volleyball. It is played with five balls and two players. Playing this game will improve your passing skills since the tosses to your partner are meant to be a bit erratic. Two jugglers face each other with an imaginary (or real) net about a foot over their heads separating them. One person has two balls and the other has three. The person with three balls starts juggling. Within seven tosses she must toss over the imaginary net. The opponent can either juggle for up to seven throws or toss one or two balls back immediately. Any ball that goes across the net must have an upward trajectory when thrown; slam dunks and smashes are not allowed. When players drop, hit the real or imaginary net, or toss out of bounds, they lose a point or the serve.

Play the game like volleyball, to a score of 15. You must win the serve before you can win a point. (One hint: If your opponent tosses two balls to you, toss two balls back, or you will be juggling four. If you toss two at once, however, they must stay within the arm span of your opponent, or you lose a point or the serve.)

Jollyball can be a crowd-pleaser for audiences, particularly in the elementary school setting. Divide your audience in half with an imaginary line down the middle. Say, "Everyone on this side of the line is for my partner, and everyone on that side of the line is for me!" Give them a very brief rundown on the rules and say that you will be playing until someone gets a score of 3. Have each side practice cheering for their champion. Then play the game fairly, but make certain that the score is 2 to 2, so you can go for game point. Really fight it out for game point, with lots of cheering on both sides. Be sure to show good sporting behavior at the end.

157 • Combat

This game was initially played with clubs, but after numerous injuries it is recommended that it be played with SuccessBalls, huge foam-filled balls with eight-inch diameters. They are available from Jugglebug (see the section at the back of this book, "Where to Go for More Information"). No matter what objects you play with, the authors take no responsibility for loosened teeth, black eyes, or bruised egos. In combat there are two important rules: First, players may not do anything that might hurt another player, and second, when you are not juggling, pick up any dropped equipment and leave the playing area until the next round.

The game is played with a large group of jugglers and is like King of the Mountain. The last player still juggling wins. Players gather in a circle and at a signal everyone starts juggling and charges onto the floor. Players try to make other players drop using any strategy. You can toss one of your balls high and knock your opponents' balls down with the other two, but you must resume juggling when your own ball comes down. You can back into other jugglers, bump them with your hips, tell a joke, or holler at them. You can even toss one of your balls away and grab an opponent's right out of the pattern without missing a beat.

Combat is a fast-moving game. Rounds often last about a minute with SuccessBalls, or five minutes with clubs, and everyone has a chance to win or be one of the last few jugglers. This game improves your reflexes, your ability to recover an erratic throw, and your peripheral vision. It is fun and exhilarating, but remember to play safe.

To a juggler, everything is a game. Passing clubs becomes the grandest game of all, especially when you create huge formations of jugglers all passing clubs to each other. In juggling, it is never about the score. Whoever has the most fun wins.

chapter

12

Performing

Juggling is a great way to make the transition from "show-off" to entertainer. If you really like attention, juggling gives you a skill that you can demonstrate to others with assurance that they will appreciate your effort. On the other hand, if you are shy, juggling can help you develop your self-confidence, knowing that you can get up and perform anytime, anywhere. If you know that you want to become a professional juggler, the chapter in *The Complete Juggler* entitled "Making Money with Juggling" has extensive details. That book and others can be found on our Web site.

Qualities of a Good Performer

The following are a few key characteristics that all great performers possess. With practice you can develop these same skills along with the confidence to put on great shows of your own.

Showmanship

Right from the start, practice being a performer. You don't have to be a great juggler to be a great entertainer. Showmanship and skill should develop hand in hand. As soon as you can do a particular move, learn to fit it into a smooth flow with another move. Instead of practicing individual skills, you then practice your routine, adding new tricks as you go along.

Learn to finish cleanly and to "style." Styling is the dramatic way you present a trick or a routine. Styling can include a flourish, a smile, raising your arms up high, even a triumphant shout. With styling even your drops can look like planned events. You can end a series of tricks with a dramatic pose that says, "You can applaud now!" Put these applause points at regular intervals throughout your routine. Remember to look at the audience and to smile.

Rhythm

Good jugglers establish a good sense of rhythm. Perform to music with a tempo and character that fit your juggling style. Swing era jazz, ragtime, symphonic overtures, TV and movie themes, circus music, or rock 'n' roll can all be appropriate. Instrumental versions are less distracting for the audience than vocal renditions.

Get a feel for the piece you want to use as your signature by juggling with it in the background. Eventually, the music will tell you when to toss wide or throw high, when to juggle small and fast, when to do a very hard trick, when to pause for applause, and when to finish with a bow. When you find a piece that fits your juggling style and character, stick with it. Adapt your tricks to the chosen music so that you are not just using it for background but are juggling with the music, tossing high on crescendos, clawing rapidly when the tempo is fast, and moving gracefully when the music is slow and lyrical.

Movement

Use your whole body and the whole stage in performance. Move from side to side, turn, spin, sit, kneel, stand, even lie down. Surprise the audience with a high throw out of a low pattern, a bounced ball that comes back again, a kicked ball, a bounce off your forehead, or a club dropped to your foot and kicked back up to the pattern. If your music is full of surprises, your juggling should be too. If your music is lyrical, or driving, or silly, your juggling should be too.

Use a video camera to record your routine and then watch it. Remember that a routine has highs and lows. Start strong with an impressive first trick, put applause points at appropriate intervals so that the audience can stay involved, and end with a crowd-pleaser so that they can show their appreciation. Have a friend videotape your performances whenever possible and make changes when necessary.

Comedic Timing

If you elect to be a comedic juggler, practice the patter as well as the patterns. Comedy requires the same level of discipline and the same attention to tempo as a musical routine, but now we call it "timing." Often, a juggling trick reminds you of something else, a yo-yo, a tennis match, a volcano. You can name these tricks aloud at the moment of audience recognition. For instance, say, "The Jugglers' Yo-Yo!" just as you begin to do it. If you start the pattern first, people may giggle, and this noise may drown out your pronouncement. If you announce the trick too soon, the element of surprise is reduced. The verbal and visual images should register on the brains of audience members simultaneously. In comedy juggling keep your words to a minimum. Remember to use funny faces, explosive noises, expressive movement, and contorted postures to reinforce moves.

Here are some additional tips for great performances:

- Develop a character that you use for juggling and choose costuming and props that work with your character. Dress unlike your audience; wear clothes that are bright and cheerful, outlandish, or elegant, but look different.

- Your routine should have a beginning, a middle, and an end and ideally tell a story. Your job is to take the audience on a pleasant journey and set them back down gently at the end.

- Face the audience whenever possible, make your movements big and showy, and use the entire stage. Juggle high and low, wide and narrow, fast and slow. Sit, kneel, lie down, leap, turn, kick or bounce a ball. Use your face and body position to express emotion. Use variety—you are a variety entertainer.

- If it is your show, make your space as theatrical as possible. Turn on the stage lights and close the curtain if one is available. If you are using an outdoor performing space, make certain the front few rows are sitting, even if it is on the grass or pavement. Even before the show begins make friends with the audience. Play pleasant and inviting music, smile, chat, shake hands, greet them as they arrive, but do not juggle in front of them before the show begins because doing so breaks the illusion and lessens the impact when they finally do see you juggle.

- When the show starts, take the stage with energy and in character. Whether you stroll shyly out in silence or run out to music, smile and look around at the audience and acknowledge them. Then get to work. Project vitality and enthusiasm with your body and your face. Smile and have fun. If you enjoy yourself, people in the audience will enjoy themselves too.

- If you work with a partner, don't upstage each other. Warm up backstage with easy skills. There should be no audible drops coming from offstage.

- If you bring volunteers on stage, make certain that they leave the stage as heroes. Never do anything to make them look bad.

- Even after you have a great routine, practice every day for at least one hour if you want to stay up with the juggling competition.

◯ Don't copy other jugglers; instead, look at other art forms for your inspiration. For example, Francis Brun, one of the idols of the juggling world, borrowed his incredible style from flamenco dancers.

Places to Perform

When you first start juggling, your audience will be your family and co-workers. You may wonder what the logical path is from that tiny captive audience to the pinnacle of performing: actually making a good living as a juggler. There is no longer a vaudeville circuit, and the few circuses that hire jugglers pay poorly and usually hire from known circus families. Nevertheless, there are many places to perform and ground rules for each.

Before we discuss some venues for performing, there are a few overall ground rules to keep in mind. First, charge money for your work. Find out what the market is in your area and price yourself appropriately. Usually this means charging more than you initially think is appropriate. Don't undersell yourself or your fellow entertainers. Dress, act, speak, and perform like a professional and you will receive a professional's fee.

◯ *Private Parties*–Birthday parties are a great way to start. If you love kids and are playful, why not give it a try. Learning a few simple magic tricks and how to tie balloon animals can help you put together an hour of material. Start with a short performance, then teach all the guests how to juggle with scarves. Use the Juggletime musical instructional audio tape, available on our Web site, to enhance your teaching. Bring peacock feathers for guests to balance and plates for them to spin also. Finish by letting the kids take the stage one by one. Give the celebrant a set of juggling scarves as a gift. Upscale private parties at country clubs or restaurants may pay a great deal more and require you only to stay in one place and juggle as "atmosphere," or to go from table to table with a close-up juggling routine.

◯ *School Assemblies*–Can you control and entertain 500 excited young-sters? Start by practicing with a single classroom, then one grade level, and finally the whole school. You need a theme or a message that is of value to educators, but if you put together a dynamic and entertaining program, you can be fully employed within an hour's drive of home. We spend an entire day in one school concluding with Family Juggling Night (figure 12.1). In this exciting day we teach scarf juggling to teachers, students, and even parents. If this sounds like a career path you want to follow, please get in touch with the authors. We can help you get trained and certified with the program we present, Juggling for Success.

◯ *Trade Shows*–At trade shows you are hired to help bring people to a booth or to bring attention to a product. You may be asked to write a routine that features your employer's product, or to teach juggling and hand out beanbag sets imprinted with your employer's logo. To work a trade show floor you need to be convivial and funny all day for several days. And you need to continually extol the virtues of your employer and their product.

○ *Public Speaking*–If you either have the ability to teach large groups to juggle with nylon scarves or can speak about self-esteem or another valued topic, you might package yourself as a public speaker. Join your local chapter of the National Speakers Association, attend their workshops, and showcase your program with them. These engagements can pay big bucks, and you may get your best bookings through speakers bureaus.

○ *Street Performing*–This venue, also including street fairs and small local festivals where they permit you to pass the hat, can be quite lucrative, but it is tough work. You must learn to gather a crowd, entertain them for no more than 20 minutes, and persuade them to pay at least one dollar per person. You will likely have to handle hecklers, drunks, and various unsavory characters. Location is everything. If you have a good spot, you can do six or eight shows in a day, work only on weekends, and make a great living.

Figure 12.1   Bright costuming and expressive movements make our Hawaiian theme a hit at school assemblies.

● *Cruise Ships, Casinos, State and County Fairs, Arts Festivals, College Circuit, Night Clubs*–If you develop an exciting, fast-paced, 20-minute comedy routine, or a 10-minute routine to music, or both, you can work these venues for the rest of your life. You will need a theatrical agent, and they can be found in the yellow pages locally or on the Internet. You'll have to create a dynamite press kit, a hot promotional video, and a Web site that really sells you. You must be a great juggler or a superior comic to thrive in this environment, as you will be competing with Russian circus performers, Chinese acrobats, comedians, and variety acts from all over the world.

Sample Routine

Now that you are developing a repertoire, why not start naming your moves as you perform. Remember to say the name of the move at the same moment you do it so that the surprising name comes just as the audience sees the move. Below is a little script you can use for your first performance. Try to visualize the moves as you read the script.

"I'm going to teach you all about juggling, a subject I'm becoming an expert on. Let's start with one ball. You don't toss it around in a circle (show the wrong way), but you toss it in a special shape. What shape do you see?" The audience will start shouting out different ideas. "It is a number." …pause… "Between seven and nine" …(Somebody says "8")… "Yes, it is an eight lying on its side, an infinity sign. First I make infinity signs over and over with one ball, then I add a second ball, and a third on this infinity sign pathway. This pattern is called the cascade; every ball goes up the center and out to the side. It is the most basic juggling pattern."

"Next, let's shift to the reverse cascade; that's where every ball goes up the outside and down the center, still infinity signs. Then come columns, where I toss one up the center and two up the side. The two can go straight up, or they can cross." (And if they bump into each other, you can say, "They can even kiss.")

"These are the basic building blocks of juggling. Now I can combine the cascade and reverse cascade—that's the half shower. I can do it from the right or from the left, and when I do it from both sides, it is called jugglers' tennis." (Run back and forth as you do the move and say, "Smash, smash, lob, lob, love 15.")

"I can juggle two in one hand or two in the other hand, and using the other ball and invisible string, I can make a yo-yo, or an oy-oy, the upside-down yo-yo. Here is the weightlifter, around the world, and the halo—Holy juggler, Batman."

"I can catch with my palm down; that's called the tax collector. Here's the tax collector in the 1800s, 'gi'me, gi'me' (claw every other ball with one hand); the 1900s, 'gi'me, gi'me, gi'me' (claw every third ball with both hands); and the tax collector for the new millennium, 'gi'me, gi'me, gi'me,

gi'me' (claw every ball with each hand). Pretty soon they'll just take it all."
(Claw all three balls in one hand and hold that hand up in the air for the
audience to see. This is your first applause point.)

"You can toss under the leg, first on one side and then on both sides. You
can throw around in a circle—that's called the shower—and when you do
it in both directions it's called the seesaw. You can toss over the shoulder
and behind the back, first on one side, and then on the other. If you really
practice hard, you can do back crosses, and when you do them, the crowd
usually goes wild. I said, 'The crowd usually goes wild.'" While you toss
successive back crosses, the crowd applauds. If they stop before you stop,
say something like, "I can juggle longer than you can clap."

"Of course you need to learn a fancy finish, and this is one of my
favorites." Go back to the cascade, toss one high in the air, and you will be
in an automatic bow when it lands in a neck catch.

"Once you can juggle with three, you can move on to four; it's just two
in each hand (demonstrate). They can go simultaneously in outside
circles, inside circles, or straight up and down. You can stagger your
throws (shift to staggered rhythm) and do the same tricks. I like to call this
one 'pistons on my old model T' (staggered columns, high and slow) or on
my new Miyata (same move, much lower and faster)." Here you might want
to catch all four and strike a victory pose with both hands in the air, or
catch one on the back of your hand and hold that hand high in the air to
signify an applause point.

"Five balls are the 'black belt' of juggling. Do you want to see five? (weak
response from audience) Do you really want to see five? (good response,
so you hold up five for them to see and take a low bow) Thank you, thank
you! … Oh, you want me to juggle them. OK, here is five the hard way (do
multiplex), five the harder way (a run of five in the cascade), and five the
hardest way." At this point you need a last, spectacular trick. You can
either shower five or do a half shower and catch them all. Or you can
simply toss one extra high, catch the other four, and then either turn a
pirouette before catching the last ball or catch the last one on the back of
your neck.

If you can pull off this sort of routine, you are ready for anything.

chapter

13

Teaching Juggling

Educators agree that students should get exercise on a regular basis right in the classroom at least once each hour, but teachers and students find that classroom calisthenics are neither fun nor easy to administer. Juggling provides a great way to solve this problem because it is classroom safe and kids love to take juggling breaks. Teachers who have used juggling for classroom activity breaks feel that it provides a "sorbet for the mind," cleaning out the cobwebs so that students can return to work refreshed.

Juggling provides a "right brain break in the left brain day" and seems to foster whole-brain learning and higher-order thinking while improving both fine and gross motor skills. Teachers report, and preliminary research confirms, that juggling helps improve handwriting, possibly because of the fine motor skills involved. It should help improve reading as well because while you are juggling you are crossing the midline and tracking, skills essential to reading. Juggling may also foster sequencing skills, the basis for math and science. So, used properly, juggling can be a powerful incentive in the classroom that can enhance the core subjects of reading, writing, math, and science. Most important, however, juggling is fun!

Effective Teaching Methods

Whether you teach a class of two or three students or a class of hundreds, there are a few techniques that will help you to be most effective.

● **Demonstrate skills step by step.** If you are an accomplished performer, resist the urge to show off for your students when you first meet them, as they may become discouraged when they see juggling as complex and difficult. At the start of the first class you may want to take a minute and merely demonstrate the cascade, reverse cascade, and columns with scarves, telling your students that these are the three building blocks to all juggling routines. After they can juggle scarves, show them the same three moves with balls. Only after they can juggle three balls in a cascade do you show them how far juggling can go. By then they will know what can be accomplished by going step by step and persevering.

● **Find personal space and organize your class.** Instruct your students to "find their personal space," a place in the room where they can spread their arms and not touch anyone else's fingertips. Have them sit. Demonstrate the first step with one object. Then, after you have given the instructions, pass out the equipment. Make this a routine they follow for every step that you teach. That way nobody is fooling around with props while you are teaching. You can use the same techniques for adults as for children.

● **Start with scarves to give students a taste of success.** Whether you are teaching at the elementary, secondary, or adult level, start with scarves. Make certain your students can juggle the cascade, columns, the reverse cascade, two in one hand, and two in the other hand before moving on to beanbags or balls. This gives them a solid repertoire, the rhythm of juggling, knowledge of the basic patterns, and a taste of success.

● **Offer help by slowing down the pattern.** When a student is struggling to master the rhythm of scarf juggling in the cascade pattern, avoid the temptation to stand behind him working his arms. Instead, stand in front and work his brain. Your job is to slow down the effects of gravity. You can simply catch the first scarf when it reaches its peak and hold it there until you see that your student has thrown the second scarf from his opposite hand and has begun to reach out with that empty hand to catch the first one. Then drop the scarf you are holding and catch and hold the second scarf with your other hand until your student has tossed the third and is ready to catch the second. In other words, you slow the pattern down to super slow motion. As your student gradually builds up speed, accommodate him by dropping scarves more and more quickly until you can step back and he can continue on his own. This same technique for slowing down the pattern can be used when teaching the cascade with beanbags or balls. Make a target for your student with your palms up, catching the ball at its peak. Then place the ball down in his hand at exactly the right moment. Once he builds up his reflexes, you can begin to drop the balls instead of handing them down.

● **Look for bad habits and correct them immediately.** When your students do move on to beanbags or balls, do not let them practice with two in one hand until they can juggle three in the cascade pattern. Otherwise, they may develop very bad habits that will be hard to break. When you teach ball juggling, of course, you start with one ball and redefine the infinity sign pathway. Then move on to two and three following the instructions in this book. However, if you find your students making mistakes or developing bad habits, there are specific remedies for each problem.

If students toss or run forward to catch, do not have them juggle against a wall. This only makes the problem worse since the wall forgives this error by bouncing the ball right back to their hands. Instead, they should visualize a wall in front of them, go back to two balls, and make certain they are tossing to two distinct peaks. With three balls they should go for three tosses, then four, forcing the balls to stay on the imaginary wall and hitting the peaks every time.

Also, with ball juggling make certain the hands stay down below the chest. If students let their hands creep higher with each toss, it speeds up the pattern and pulls them forward.

Many people have practiced wrong in the past and have built up a bad habit. They hand across in a two-ball shower pattern, with the dominant hand doing all the tossing and the nondominant hand merely pushing across. If this is the case, stop the students immediately and have them start with two balls in their nondominant hand. Once that hand gets used to tossing, the problem usually evaporates.

● **Explain juggling as a series of right-left units for proper rhythm.** If students toss two beanbags at the same time, one from each hand, tell them to wait until #1 gets to the top before tossing #2. You may have to restrain one hand a bit to get the rhythm right. The opposite problem is when they toss too late, just before a ball hits their hand. In either case, make certain they use every peak as a cue to toss another ball.

As soon as you can, get your students to think not in terms of "1, 2, 3, 4..." but in terms of "1, 2, 1, 2..." or "right, left, right, left...." Continuation is a great deal easier when you think about juggling as a series of right-left units, not as a succession of individual tosses.

○ **Keep these helpful tips in mind when working with large groups:**

1. Warm everyone up with a few minutes of stretching before class.
2. Sit students on the floor with their equipment on the ground behind their backs.
3. Give the instructions for the next move when everyone is sitting.
4. Have them mime the juggling moves with empty hands.
5. Have them repeat your verbal cues.
6. Turn on the music and have your students stand up and practice.
7. Constantly remind them that a drop is a sign of progress, and that they learn to juggle drop by drop.

Every time you and your students get together, have them practice everything they've learned so far before you teach a new trick. This way, they can get limbered up and they won't forget their previous tricks and building blocks. If a few of your students are struggling, focus on them and let the others charge ahead and try new tricks. You'll spend 80 percent of your time on 20 percent of your students, but the others don't need you as much. Your most effective coaching tool for these struggling students is praise.

Monitoring and Encouraging Progress

On the wall of your practice space put up poster boards labeled Scarf Cascade, Columns, Reverse Cascade, Scarf Master, Ball Cascade, and Ball Master. Give each of your students a sticky note with their full name printed on it in big block letters. Move their sticky note up the progression of charts as they conquer each level.

Encourage students to record their progress every day. They can list skills they are working on down the left side of a sheet of graph paper and the dates along the top. Then every day have them aim to exceed the number of tosses and catches for each skill and record their best score for each skill in the appropriate box. As soon as they get 100 repetitions with a skill, they can cross it off the list and put on another one.

If you like to see lightbulbs go on over students' heads as they burst through to successful juggling, you may want to teach juggling either for fun or profit. To practice your technique, you can offer to teach juggling to your local scout troop, Boys and Girls Club, park and recreation department, or health club. Start with scarves and go step by step as you did in this book. Eventually, just as the senior author did, you may decide to "jump ship" and start teaching juggling for a living. For detailed lesson plans and in-depth information on teaching juggling professionally, look at the chapter on teaching juggling in *The Complete Juggler*, available on our Web site.

Where to Go for More Information

Juggling—*From Start to Star* is not intended to be exhaustive. If you work your way through this book and still need more fuel for your juggling fire, consider our 575-page book, *The Complete Juggler,* an exhaustive body of information by the senior author, or our two-hour instructional video, *Juggling Step by Step.* For beginning and intermediate juggling props, look for the Jugglebug brand at your local magic store, kite shop, or mom and pop toy store, or on the Web at **www.jugglebug.com**. To get beginning juggling equipment in quantity for a store, a school, or a recreation program, your best source is Sportime at 1-800-444-5700 or on the Web at **www.sportime.com**.

To get detailed video instruction on the moves in this book and many other tricks as well, or to find out about starting a juggling program in your school or summer camp, please visit the web site of Juggling for Success, our non-profit affiliate, at **www.jugglingforsuccess.org**. From either of our sites you can link up with the International Jugglers' Association (IJA), publisher of *JUGGLE* magazine and sponsor of the IJA Festival, an annual gathering of over 1,000 jugglers held in North America. You can also link to the Juggling Information Service where you can find out about juggling activities and local and regional festivals in your area, and can network with professional and recreational jugglers and prop makers worldwide. Through our web sites you can also find out about the European Juggling Association. European activities are outlined in the magazine *Kaskade* which is published in English and German. As activities develop elsewhere in the world of juggling we will continue to create links for jugglers at our web sites.

About the Authors

Dave, Dorothy, and Ben are father, daughter, and son in the famous juggling Finnigan family. All are amazingly talented at juggling, and all have performed their craft before audiences throughout the country.

Dave Finnigan is the former education director of the International Jugglers Association (IJA) and was the first-ever recipient of the IJA's Excellence in Education Award. He is also the author of *The Complete Juggler* and *The Joy of Juggling,* and a prolific showman and highly respected instructor. Since 1976 he has visited more than 2,000 schools and taught more than a million people in 41 states and 12 countries to juggle. Dave is well known for incorporating a variety of teaching styles and uses those techniques to help children learn, while at the same time encouraging a positive self-image.

Dorothy Finnigan, at age 17, is one of the most accomplished female jugglers in the United States. She has personally taught thousands of children and adults to juggle in her travels. She was also the winner of the Most Promising Woman Award from the IJA in 1997 and in Montreal in 2000 was the first female ever to receive a medal in the IJA junior competition.

Ben Finnigan, age 13, is also an up-and-coming star in the world of juggling. Ben claims to be as good a juggler at 13 as his father was at 36, or is at 59. Although he is a member of a juggling family, Ben always reminds everyone that he is "just a regular kid" and living proof that anyone, young or old, can learn to juggle with the right instruction.